T0155641

Fashion Tech Applied

Exploring Augmented Reality, Artificial Intelligence, Virtual Reality, NFTs, Body Scanning, 3D Digital Design, and More

Von N. Ruzive
Peter Jeun Ho Tsang

Apress®

Fashion Tech Applied: Exploring Augmented Reality, Artificial Intelligence, Virtual Reality, NFTs, Body Scanning, 3D Digital Design, and More

Von N. Ruzive
Paris, France

Peter Jeun Ho Tsang
Paris, France

ISBN-13 (pbk): 978-1-4842-9693-6
https://doi.org/10.1007/978-1-4842-9694-3

ISBN-13 (electronic): 978-1-4842-9694-3

Managing Director, Apress Media LLC: Welmoed Spahr
Acquisitions Editor: Miriam Haidara
Development Editor: James Markham
Project Manager: Jessica Vakili

Distributed to the book trade worldwide by Springer Science+Business Media New York, 1 NY PLaza, New York, NY 10004. Phone 1-800-SPRINGER, fax (201) 348-4505, e-mail orders-ny@springer-sbm.com, or visit www.springeronline.com. Apress Media, LLC is a California LLC and the sole member (owner) is Springer Science + Business Media Finance Inc (SSBM Finance Inc). SSBM Finance Inc is a **Delaware** corporation.

For information on translations, please e-mail booktranslations@springernature.com; for reprint, paperback, or audio rights, please e-mail bookpermissions@springernature.com.

Apress titles may be purchased in bulk for academic, corporate, or promotional use. eBook versions and licenses are also available for most titles. For more information, reference our Print and eBook Bulk Sales web page at http://www.apress.com/bulk-sales.

Any source code or other supplementary material referenced by the author in this book is available to readers on the Github repository: https://github.com/Apress/Applying-Fashion-Tech. For more detailed information, please visit https://www.apress.com/gp/services/source-code.

Paper in this product is recyclable.

Dedicated to fashion, tech, and supply chain enthusiasts who want to dive deeper to break norms of the fashion industry.

Table of Contents

TABLE OF CONTENTS

About the Authors

Von N. Ruzive is a fashion tech and inclusivity consultant particularly working with brands and startups. She has focused on unconventional ways to transform the fashion industry through technology and universal design while teaching these topics to master's and bachelor's programs in Paris. Von has also launched Foundry Powered By IFA Paris with the IFA Paris team in 2019 - a fashion incubator program and fashion tech innovation lab in Paris.

Peter Jeun Ho Tsang is the founder and CEO of Beyond Form, a fashion tech venture studio. Since obtaining a master's degree in Digital Fashion from London College of Fashion in the late 2000s, he has developed several fashion tech initiatives including a retail store of the future in London, a lab in Paris, and an MBA program. At Beyond Form, he now works with entrepreneurs globally to build and scale technology solutions for the fashion industry.

About the Technical Reviewer

Melissa A. Borza is Vice President, Strategy and Marketing, at Netformx. Before joining Netformx, she worked as a product leader at CA Technologies. Prior to that, she worked as a journalist and technical writer. Melissa has taught technical writing, public speaking, and product management classes and is a member of the Society of Children's Book Writers and Illustrators. She presents regularly at conferences around the world, such as the Grace Hopper Celebration of Women in Computing, and she contributes frequent articles and blogs on change management, team transformations, product management, and increasing the representation of women in IT and other STEM careers. Melissa holds a patent in an integrated impact analysis system. She earned her MA in Communications from Syracuse University and her BA in English and Psychology from Cornell University.

Acknowledgments

Von N. Ruzive: Throughout my journey of working in the fashion tech world, I have had the chance to meet phenomenal industry experts and enthusiasts, who have contributed greatly to my professional experiences thus far. I am grateful for all of the insights and support from all of you throughout all of my professional ventures, including this book. I look forward to continuously push boundaries in the industry together in Paris and beyond. I couldn't complete this book without mentioning my husband, Steph - you consistently cheer me on and I remain thankful, you made the writing of this book possible for me.

Peter Jeun Ho Tsang: Fashion tech has come a long way since I started studying the subject over a decade ago. I'd like to thank everyone that has helped me on this journey so far: my business partners supporting the builds of Beyond Form, Foundry Powered by IFA Paris, and The Dandy Lab; the incredible entrepreneurs and startups whom are constantly pushing me to think outside the box daily; mentors and cheerleaders from academia to industry experts; and to all that have helped me to launch fashion tech projects in Paris - my home away from the UK. Thanks to you, I'm filled with experiences that have helped shape this book.

Preface

Fashion tech – a term that remains enigmatic even to the fashion professionals. It's almost like a verb that only those in the space are slowly understanding how to do – or at least think they know. From the new generation of materials to digital fashion NFTs, the shift in fashion is becoming more mainstream as you read this book. That's good news for tech companies that can now implement their expertise into the fashion industry.

Fashion was once a traditional playing field with pretty much one way of working – as a brand, a linear way of following the process from designing all the way to selling. Now? Brick-and-mortar stores are no longer the go-to for all fashion retail, which opens up a whole new role for online stores and a place for convenience, ease, and faster access to a world full of products online and Web3. Brands also no longer need to follow the traditional supply chain throughout.

From this, a spiral effect has happened where fashion tech once was known as just a space for wearables but now geared toward all sorts of solutions to combat the challenges of the industry across the supply chain. Product sizing, and lack of traceability are among the issues that companies are focusing on resolving for consumers with their innovations. These efforts are reshaping business models in hope to match the consumers of today who can never have enough convenience.

Many tech startups are also considering ways for fashion brands and retailers to be more cost and time efficient with their technologies. Having her own inclusive womenswear clothing brand and worked with various fashion brands, Von understands the need to collaborate with other expertise to achieve innovation in what is already a saturated industry. After exploring the more retail side of innovation with the use of augmented reality to present her clothing, this was just the first of many partnerships to see firsthand what technology can offer when implemented into a fashion brand.

With experience working in conventional methods of the value chain in established fashion brands such as French Connection and Y/Project and understanding the traditional fashion schooling deeper, Von has been teaching unconventional modules to the next generation of fashion students in Paris. With a lens on breaking the norms of fashion, the subjects Von has taught have included reconsidering prosthetics and footwear through 3D modeling and additive manufacturing, to considering different body types when designing garments in 3D digital software in partnership with Global Brands Group, with Master and Bachelor students. 2019 was then the year Von launched the Foundry Powered by IFA Paris fashion incubator program and fashion innovation lab with the IFA Paris team, which began as a fashion tech specialized program, and was how Von & Peter met. Together they supported fashion tech startups and connected them with industry fashion brands who share a thirst for innovation.

Rewind to the late 2000s and fashion tech was still a noncategory for many fashion brands, professionals, and fashion schools. Having studied digital fashion at the London College of Fashion around this period, Peter saw where technology could have an impact on fashion. Although technologies such as 3D fashion and visualization were still clunky, data was hardly leveraged, and blockchain was still only in its early research phase, the beginnings of fashion tech started to shape new types of conversations around fashion and innovation.

A lot has happened since then in the world of technology, and the aforementioned subjects are now mainstay topics of conversation for many in and out of the industry. 2015 saw Peter launch his first retail tech lab in London that explored what the future of physical retail may look like.

Experiential retail, in-store iBeacon-enabled journeys, and app-enabled conveniences such as queue-free payment systems drove his first body of work exploring how tech could create a shift in industry practices. The project, perhaps a little ahead of its time, informed his next iteration of innovation building. Beyond Form, a venture studio building fashion tech startups, uses continual learnings to bring nascent ideas to fruition. This is done by operational support and financing.

Since launching our work with fashion tech startups in 2020, we've seen the sector move at lightning speed and the fashion industry finally coming around to the idea that technology and innovation are hyper-enablers to solve many of the industry's challenges.

It's not possible to envision a transformation of the fashion industry without understanding the starting points. This is where education plays an active role in nurturing the future of fashion tech. Either through schools teaching new ways to innovate or by reading this book, it is important to understand the fundamentals of what consists a fashion supply chain, the processes, and finally how technology has been used so far to how it can be pushed even further later on.

This book aims to dissect some of the main challenges that will inevitably impact the global system and the macro issues such as climate change, overconsumption, and borderless commerce. With a particular focus on apparel, each section of this book will put a lens on the existing conventions practiced in the industry and how innovations such as augmented reality, artificial intelligence, virtual reality, NFTs, body scanning, 3D digital design, and more could completely revolutionize how you approach and solve challenges in fashion.

We've worked with ambitious founders from around the world, from Vietnam to Canada, and many countries in between. Interestingly, most of the founders do not have a fashion background but have identified challenges that can be turned into opportunities. What this signifies is that the fashion industry is ripe for disruption; however, it takes these outsiders too long to learn about the industry in order to create compelling fashion tech solutions quickly enough. As timing is everything with tech and fashion, this book exists to bring readers up to speed with the foundations of the subject and how the two industries collide – this means from theoretical and practical application perspectives.

The application of technology into the fashion industry is what the reader should be able to take away from this book. This includes the identification of suitable tools, how they can be integrated into the fashion business, and what outcomes could be expected. Most importantly, understanding that the future of the fashion industry and its continual impact on people's lives and the planet will pan out with significant influence from innovations that may not even exist yet. We recommend at the end of each chapter to explore the activities suggested to take a deeper dive on that subject by accessing all links via the QR code. Since the industry is so large and there are so many technologies now applicable to it, it's not possible to talk about all of them in this book. However, we hope that this is the first stepping stone for your interest into the world of fashion tech.

QR CODE: Use this QR code to access links referenced through the book.

CHAPTER 1

Introduction to Fashion Technology

1.1. The Fashion Value Chain

Before we can understand how technology is having a significant role in transforming the fashion industry, we need to lay out the foundations of how the system is built. Traditionally the fashion value chain has looked something like Figure 1-1.

Figure 1-1. *The linear fashion value chain*

A linear system whereby products are created by fashion brands and retailers for consumers to use and then dispose of, most commonly into the landfill. Value is extracted by taking resources at cost price, a markup or profit margin is applied on top, and then products are sold to the customer for the end retail price. A simple business model that the industry has built most of its three trillion USD market value on (CB Insights, 2022) and continues to do so at present. This applies to all market levels, from mass market right through to luxury and in all forms of product creations from ready to wear to bespoke.

Fashion is one of the major global industries, and since it is so large, there are many challenges that are presented across the value chain. Some of these challenges technology can help to solve at speed, but technology can't solve every issue in the industry due to how fashion businesses are structured, for example, cultural traditions and processes such as in the design and development department that are baked into the core of a company, or modern consumption habits of the everyday customer. These challenges paired with executive managers struggling to guide their companies into the next tech-enabled era have caused them to simply go out of business. This was demonstrated significantly during the COVID-19 pandemic of 2020 and 2021 that saw the collapse of large empires including Arcadia Group (Topshop, Topman, Miss Selfridge, etc.) and Debenhams in the UK and Lord & Taylor in the United States. We can break down the value chain to understand where some of the sticking points are.

1.1.1. Concept Creation and Design

The start of the value chain is where fashion concepts are conjured up and is undeniably the most creative part of the fashion value chain. Here, creative directors, fashion designers, and product developers build collections and product ranges to be pushed through the rest of the value chain. Having trained as fashion designers ourselves, we understand that creation is an emotional and messy process with the paradigm of "design" quite often subjective.

Since the process of concept and design creation is extremely personal, it has meant that the start of the value chain has been disrupted the least by technology to date. Many industry professionals believe that creativity cannot be replicated, aided, or replaced, thus creating a resistant mindset: *"[Fashion] educators say students are so far not rushing to embrace the [generative AI] technology, however, as many want to learn traditional techniques or fear the unknown"* (Bain, 2023). This mindset has led to a traditional culture being maintained within the product design and development business functions. Although problematic because many fashion brands are hiring for roles that require new technical skill sets, many designers are slowly adopting innovations within their processes. Within recent years, this has not been more evident than with digital fashion and 3D digital prototyping, which accelerated at lightning speed since 2020. Brands such as Nike, Adidas, Hugo Boss, and Tommy Hilfiger have created digital fashion departments to support the role of traditional fashion design. We'll explore more what the future design workforce looks like in Chapter 2.

Startups such as The Fabricant and RTFKT have brought digital fashion to the forefront for both the industry and the general consumer. The Fabricant specifically is democratizing fashion design with their co-creation platform, in which anyone can now create a piece of digital fashion. However, this is not the only way the role of the designer is changing. Artificial intelligence has made it possible to back design decisions using AI-generated trend forecasts based on various data points including e-commerce sites, social media, and brand-owned CRM systems. Companies such as T-Fashion, Heuritech, and StyleSage offer such solutions. This can be taken even one step further with generative design, or generative adversarial network (GAN), whereby a computer can now design full collections with simple prompts from a human. Although still nascent, this creates a conversation on the role of the designer-developer in the future.

1.1.2. Prototyping and Manufacturing

The production phase of the value chain is where products come into existence. The global supply chain of the fashion industry touches every corner of the planet and affects millions of people's livelihoods. The sheer scale on which this part of the value chain operates has the biggest impact on the Earth and has the greatest need for transformation, mostly due to the unsustainable practices that it presents. It is also the hardest part for fashion tech to penetrate because it mainly consists of hard technologies (physical technologies such as computers, machinery, and production tools) that have high costs and long timelines to roll out, couple this with the fact that most brands do not own their supply chain and rely on a network of third-party suppliers to bring everything together. High collaboration is needed in a space where there is little worldwide governance. However, many daring startup founders and government organizations are rapidly changing this, which we'll explore more in Chapter 3.

The Fourth Industrial Revolution, a term coined in 2016 by Klaus Schwab, Founder and Executive Chairman of the World Economic Forum, describes the age that we are living in. Digitalization, connectivity, and hyper-speed realities are causing fashion manufacturing to change. Only ten years ago it was nearly impossible for an industry outsider to produce a collection at small scale, to the right quality, and instantly. However, with the dawn of the Fourth Industrial Revolution, on-demand manufacturing has been made possible with platforms such as PlatformE, supplier databases such as Material Exchange, and marketplaces such as Queen of Raw. Digital authentication, transparency tech, and blockchain are augmenting this for brands small and large to produce with conscientiousness and an awareness of the origins of their products.

As hard tech is also becoming more advanced and accessible, tech such as 3D printing, laser cutting, and body scanning is changing the way designers are creating their collections. Designer Iris van Herpen is one outstanding example of where technology, creativity, and engineering have harmonized to create beautiful objects that go beyond fashion. She has inspired many others to push the boundaries of what physical production can do with these technologies.

However, the fashion supply chain is still a behemoth yet still to be overcome, and startups are developing tech such as digital IDs, blockchain product authentication, and RFID-enabled threads and powders. Although the surface has barely been touched, the building blocks are being put in place, especially with the backing of organizations like the H&M Foundation and Fashion for Good.

1.1.3. Marketing and Showcasing/Retail and Distribution

The downstream phase of the fashion value chain, which entails everything from marketing, showcasing, warehousing, logistics, and of course offline and online retailing, this part of the value chain has been transformed by modern innovations the most. Both online and offline retailing have had significant advances, from retail store formats to experiences and from clientele services to omnichannel; retail is being transformed at a fundamental level that the other parts of the value chain are yet to experience. Tangible changes over the last 10–15 years have included foundational technologies that help the industry to run such as digital showrooms and AI-powered and data-driven personalized shopping and product authentication. Consumer-facing tech has been polished to a high level including augmented reality experiences, in-store efficiency tools such as queue-less payment systems, as well as the flashier tech such as magic mirrors that nobody seems to have gotten 100% completely right yet.

The business model of fashion retail has also benefited from tech, which has significantly allowed it to change. Traditionally, many new and small to medium-sized brands relied on a network of wholesale partners to distribute their products such as sales agents, department stores, and independent boutiques. Therefore, a business-to-business (B2B) model that requires a wholesale price and a retail price, which means a game of profit margins. However, with the dawn of Shopify and more sophisticated web tools and social media, direct to consumer (D2C) has proliferated since the early 2010s. Stitch Fix is a great example of a quasi-brand and online retailer that has successfully utilized data, web, and AI to sell personalized products and subscription boxes to the consumer directly without the aid of an intermediary. Likewise, retailers such as Farfetch have opened an entire world to brands and boutiques from around the world to new consumers that were previously extremely difficult for them to reach because of logistics. This D2C model has allowed greater flexibility with margins, control of prices and products, and the overall shopping experience. Thus, many previous retailing barriers are instantly removed for fledgling brands.

Since online shopping has increased vastly across desktop and mobile devices, and soon within the metaverse too, retail tech has been given plenty of opportunities to innovate. Discovery tech such as automated fashion stylists, fit tech like virtual try-ons and fit finders, shoppable media content and live streaming, and gamified shopping apps have enriched the shopping journey from start to finish. Consumers are now expecting their favorite shopping destinations to give them more than just a transactional portal. As demonstrated by the COVID-19 pandemic high street clean out, retailers that went bankrupt or struggled were the ones that did not adopt technologies into their core businesses.

However, this is not to say that physical retailing is dying, but retailers are being forced to rethink their retail formats to meet consumer expectations. For example, the Amazon Style store that was launched in May 2022 in Los Angeles is an experimental store loaded with tech and optimized shopping tricks. Farfetch's pop-up store of the future in 2017 leaned toward the thinking that all stores will eventually be like a computer operating system whereby different pieces of technology can be plugged in, launched, and plugged out at will to meet the shopping experience demands. Peter's previous business, The Dandy Lab, explored several "future store" themes including physical retail as media, plug-and-play store fitouts, and online to offline experiences, which echoed the possibilities of what in-store formats could be. The Dandy Lab had several pop-up sites between 2014 and 2017 (Figures 1-2a, 1-2b, 1-2c), which at this period the hype of fashion and retail tech was starting to pick up.

Figure 1-2a. *The Dandy Lab Bird Street with Pavegen technology*

Figure 1-2b. *The Dandy Lab Bird Street with magic mirror technology*

Figure 1-2c. *The Dandy Lab Spitalfields with interactive screens and NFC storytelling*

1.1.4. End Customer and End of Life

It is no surprise that with the advancements of technology comes the evolution of the consumer. This means an evolution of their tastes, expectations, behaviors, demands, desires, needs, and their general attitudes toward fashion. Fashion for themselves as a customer, but also their views on the industry at large and what it means in the wider context of the planet and society. Just as technology is rapidly changing, so are consumption patterns. The end customer is the driver for the value chain, where retailers and brands are fighting for revenue in a market landscape of plentiful fashion options. This is where tech-enabled retail formats, digital-forward omnichannel touch points, and social commerce are key in capturing customer attention. In Chapters 4 and 5, we'll explore what happens (or isn't happening) once customers have finished using their products.

However, getting customers to spend their cash isn't the only important factor. With climate crisis issues coming to the forefront in recent years, issues such as sustainability, transparency, and traceability, once associated with hippies and vegans as recently as the late 2000s, have filtered into present mainstream consumption. Thus, it has given innovations an opportunity at the end of the value chain to come to life. We can call this the end-of-life phase of the product life cycle.

The three R's: rental, repair, and resale. Each one of the 3 R's has given life to platforms such as Rent the Runway, Save Your Wardrobe, and Vestiaire Collective, respectively, that have managed to develop sophisticated logistics and operational efficiencies to deliver seamless experiences allowing the customer to consume in an eco-friendlier way, thus combatting the fashion industry's penchant for overproduction and encouragement of overconsumption. Some of these platforms have become huge globally, which demonstrates the customer's heightened awareness of the industry's impact on the environment.

As with the business model of retailing changing, ownership is also changing. Consumers are now more than happy to rent items or sell unwanted goods: "1 in 3 apparel items bought in the last 12 months was secondhand…64% say they [Gen Z] look for an item secondhand before buying it new" (threadUP, 2023). StockX, a trading platform for sneakers, paved the way for consumer-to-consumer transactions likened to that of the financial industry. Marketplaces in general have proliferated and enabled consumers to engage, trade, and be part of communities that are tapping into product niches, new product categories, and alternative assets. NFTs (non-fungible tokens), although nascent, shift the paradigm of where value lies within a product. Since the 2020s began, digital fashion has come to the forefront as an asset that fashion consumers are wanting to purchase and own, which may or may not be associated with a physical product and brand experience.

Ultimately, the end customer no longer just wants goods pushed onto them through glossy fashion magazines or marketing campaigns, but a much more diverse way of consuming fashion. With this shift, fashion tech can tap into unchartered territories that many fashion brands and retailers have yet to explore.

1.1.5. What the Fashion Value Chain Looks Like Moving Forward

What we can delineate with the dawn of the fashion tech revolution is that the old fashion system is no longer set up for modern society. Disruption across the entire value chain is underway, which presents exciting things ahead. One way that we can tangibly see this is by the industry (very) slowly transforming its value chain from a linear into a circular system. It looks something like Figure 1-3.

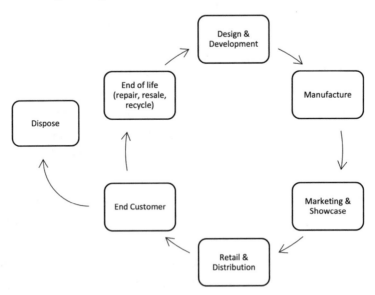

Figure 1-3. *Circular Fashion model*

The circular system does highlight that value is no longer just created by the brand, nor is value captured just in the initial sale of a product. Brands no longer hold the power that they once did to control every aspect of the value chain, which is instigating some interesting adaptations. Customers are also now designers, makers, creators, sellers, and buyers with the ability to assimilate between each role with ease using an arsenal of fashion technologies. For example, they may want to upcycle their existing wardrobe to be sold on a social marketplace like Depop. Perhaps they may also want to design their own digital fashion collection to be minted into NFTs to be sold on The Fabricant, which can then be taken into the metaverse for showcasing in Decentraland. Finally, if they choose to do so, they can create one-off garments, on demand, using platforms such as Drippy that have no minimum order quantities. The possibilities are endless.

For the industry, untapped or lost value is there along the value chain. Deadstock fabrics and unsold goods are two examples of where tech can help to unlock this value by either being transformed into new goods or managed efficiently to extract value in a different manner. Additionally, most brands don't know what happens to their products once they have been sold and therefore miss the opportunity to extend the brand experience beyond the final sale. Digital product passports and IDs, verified on blockchain, allow brands and users to follow the life of a product from one user to the next, thus either extracting further value in the form of royalty fees or resale credits, offering extended brand experiences or content, or recirculating a used item on an own-brand rental or resale platform. This ultimately means that innovations are allowing brands to extract value and chase opportunities in areas not previously looked at.

The fashion value chain also does not have to stay with just physical products; digital assets are being explored. Nike's acquisition of digital fashion startup RTFKT at the end of 2021 signaled to the industry and beyond that digital assets are going to be an important aspect of value creation. Just as how fashion and music industries collided in the early

2000s, fashion and gaming are now in an intimate dance with each other. Brands such as Gucci, Prada, and Balenciaga have all explored ways to integrate gaming and gamification into their brands with either stand-alone campaigns or collaborations in well-established computer games such as Halo and Fortnite. By doing so, a whole new world is opened up for opportunities to be taken in which some digital assets are selling for more than $1 million per item.

What we will explore later in this book is to just what extent the narrative between brand and consumer has been changed throughout the various phases of the value chain through technology. We will also discover how these technologies can be implemented for different purposes into a brand's business model – it's a lot more than people realize.

1.2. The Role and Impact of Technology

Throughout history, technology has been one of the key accelerators and indicators for the evolution of human civilization. It has touched every facet of human life, from agriculture to communication, from education to mobility, and more. Although taken for granted in modern times, for ancient civilizations, the dawn of technologies as simple as glass and irrigation systems meant that populations were able to build cities and empires that were able to support life beyond what was previously possible. As with all advancements, it comes with positive and negative impacts, but more importantly technology has enabled the shaping of society in many ways. For fashion, this has meant the rapid globalization of the industry with mega brands and conglomerates forming, fast fashion coming into prevalence, and digitally native vertical brands (DNVB) reaching unique demographics with products crafted specifically just for them.

From an industrialization perspective, technology has had a huge direct impact in the fundamental ways we design, produce, and sell products. The main ways include the following:

- Efficiencies: Many aspects of the supply chain have already been automated, such as that of stock management, warehousing, and buying. This has meant fewer human errors, higher accuracies in predicted stock levels, and less faulty products being produced. Although not quite there yet, fully automated factories without human intervention will be possible in the future. Softwear Automation and Sewbo are two examples of companies exploring how to get sewing robots to fully craft a garment. The result is not at commercial scale yet, but given the pace of the advancements, more robots will be integrated into the fashion supply chain within the next 10–15 years.

- Speed and time: Digitalization of fashion has meant that information and assets are now transmitted at the click of a button. Gone are the days of needing to send a paper sewing pattern or a technical pack by traditional courier, designs can now be approved by digital prototypes, and trims can be printed on demand to specification. Processes for many job roles across the value chain have sped up, which has meant that value creation and value-added activities are the main driving forces for brands.

- Cost: Fashion has never been cheaper before. This is partly due to offshore manufacturing in developing countries and the other part being modern innovations allowing products to be manufactured at scale using relatively inexpensive materials. Materials innovations, advanced machinery, and sophisticated product lifecycle management (PLM) systems such as those developed by Lectra have meant the sum of efficiency, speed, and time has drastically reduced product development and manufacturing costs.

- Reach: The Internet has meant that the business of fashion can now be done from anywhere in the world. The young entrepreneur based in New York City can now get their collection prototyped on demand in Vietnam using a supply chain management platform such as Inflow. The small independent boutique in Los Angeles can now reach even more customers by connecting their physical store to online connector platforms such as Farfetch, who can then also handle all their international logistics. Reach is no longer a problem, but how you do it is what will make or break a brand.

As well as the back end of fashion being greatly affected, technological advancements have had a major impact on society. This includes the following:

- Life span: The product life cycle, either being thrown away or put back into the system for second use, has shortened. This applies to not only basics and fast fashion but throughout all the different market levels (bar haute couture). Throwaway culture and instant fashion have risen to the forefront over the last 40 years because of the advancement of technologies enabling these aspects. This shows the negative and positive sides of tech's role in modernization of an industry.

- Commoditization of fashion: Most brands are just churning out stuff and at speed. Rising costs, economic downturns, and increased competition have led the shift to decrease in value of fashion. As a result, generic products, perpetual discounting, and increased sheer volume of different products available have created overconsumption. Amazon Fashion and Amazon Marketplace are examples whereby sophisticated algorithms and logistics have made it even easier for people to churn out stuff and for people to consume it. Now it's necessary for fashion tech to try to combat this huge consumer behavioral problem.

- Democratization of fashion: The customer can now also be the designer with co-creation integrations like PlatformE. Brands are now created by the everyday person on platforms like CALA. Retailers are online stores run by influencers on social commerce platforms such as The List. Fashion is truly democratized, which is great but also presents a variety of challenges as well as opportunities.

1.2.1. The Next Industrial Revolution

Most of us don't realize but we are in the middle of a revolution. Marc Andreessen, an entrepreneur and investor, said back in 2011 "software is eating the world," (Andreessen, 2011) predicting that software would disrupt traditional industries and essentially transform the core of how they operate and along with it bring a plethora of opportunities. What Uber has done for mobility, and Airbnb has done for tourism, companies such as Rent the Runway, Lyst, and Depop are doing for fashion.

Although fashion was late to the digitalization party, once it caught up, there have been dramatic changes across the entire value chain for both back-end and front-end use cases. Throughout fashion's history, each revolution has had a huge evolutionary impact. The first industrial revolution saw machines being introduced that turned garment making from handmade and slow to speed – think the automated loom and of course the sewing machine. As humans began to harness electricity, this meant that machines could be sped up further, thus creating efficiencies and the ability to have mass production. Third and fourth revolutions have all been about the computer and the digital age, and ultimately transforming the entire industry.

64.6% of the world's population is connected to the Internet (Statista, 2023). In a short space of time, fashion's entire supply chain has been connected. Communication and collaboration can be done with ease, which has seen many processes such as digital and rapid prototyping take off. When Peter was starting out in production in China, digital fabric printing used to be expensive, costing a minimum of around $10 per meter. Fast-forward to present day and the same process can now cost less than $1 per meter depending on the final finish and fabric. Interesting collaborations such as Adidas and Carbon launched their Futurecraft 3D-printed shoe in 2018, demonstrating the possibilities of advanced fashion tech. The Futurecraft shoe is not yet widely available but does indicate where the industry will be heading – products that are hyper-adapted to the wearer, printed on demand, and evolved to the customer's every need.

Although in its infancy, the world is shifting into the next industrial revolution: the fifth one. An era where humans and machines will exist symbiotically and the lines between the two become even blurrier. This revolution will reconfigure human civilization once again. Artificial intelligence will greatly take over the thought processes of man (not to say that we will become lazy) and allow us to achieve activities at explosive speeds and at much greater scales. For fashion, this will mean generative design will come to realization where AI can predict, create, and produce fashion all by itself. Product, overlaid by tech, will become a super second skin on the body, thus allowing us to achieve tasks that are beyond our normal states. Materials will be able to grow out of virtually nothing as well as self-generate and ultimately remove our heavy reliance on man-made fibers. Finally, shopping experiences will mean every touch point is personalized and products are augmented to the individual. Side note: Augmented products is a term utilized in fashion business and retail that denotes the differentiation of products from one brand to the next through additional features, add-ons, and services, for example, an NFT that is delivered with a purchased physical product that allows the customer to gain exclusive brand benefits and experiences.

1.2.2. The Next Wave of Tech

Since technologies come and go, it's more pertinent to understand the macro mega-trends that will affect the fashion industry rather than focusing on any single technology. These trends indicate the next technologies that will come into our lives and ultimately change the fashion landscape. Undoubtedly, tech advancements are only speeding up faster, which means that we are going to see changes from an industrial and consumer perspective at a quick pace. By 2030, the modern day will look vastly different from the present day and add a further ten years to 2040, and it'll look different even further. Some of the highlights include the following:

> Web 3.0: The Internet is heading into its fifth
> decade of existence and transitioning into its third
> iteration – a decentralized ecosystem. Powered by
> tech such as blockchain and AI, the Internet will be
> able to process information in a smart human-
> like way. For fashion, it means digital assets and

experiences executed in new ways, whereby users can own digital fashion that also unlocks physical experiences. Independent creators can make money in new novelty ways, and the brands are able to engage with customers on platforms yet to be utilized by fashion, for example, gaming worlds and Discord communities. Since Web 3.0 is meant to be amorphous, it will force fashion to shape-shift along with how the Internet (currently Web 2.0) will eventually change.

Automation and data: It's estimated that 18% of the global labor workforce could be automated according to Goldman Sachs (Briggs and Kodnani, 2023), with countries including the United States, UK, Japan, and Hong Kong potentially seeing the highest rates. Blue- and white-collar jobs will significantly change over the next few decades as brands get to grips with leveraging their proprietary data. What's exciting though, tasks such as collection design and planning will be fully assisted by AI. The fashion designer will never lose their creativity but will be able to validate their ideas using analytics tools, or even ask the computer to help them to design. Although this will be scary at first, eventually the boundaries of creation and fashion will be pushed once humans learn how to fully capitalize on AI. We'll see many examples of this happening across the value chain, which we're already seeing beginning to happen across retail touch points. Everyone now appreciates when a service is personalized to their individual needs.

Trust and transparency: Let's be frank here; if a brand can't build trust, then said brand is unlikely to grow. This is where blockchain technology can really help to build trust by offering uncorrupted information about where products come from and how they pass through the value chain. Brands will be able to authenticate every piece of data and utilize that in a meaningful way with the end customer. As we've also seen in the last decade, what it means to own fashion has also changed, with recommerce platforms such as Vestiaire Collective and thredUP proliferating. Therefore, trust will not only mean business to customer (B2C), but also from customer to customer (C2C) and having ownership authenticated. This may not mean much for low-ticket items, but for luxury, this will mean services, interaction, and engagement further beyond the initial transaction.

Next-generation materials: Materials, one of the fundamentals of the fashion industry and yet one of the hardest parts to advance. This is because of long research and development times and difficulty to scale commercially. Costs paired with hard tech that needs to be built mean that next-generation materials have an extremely high barrier to get integrated into the system. However, with materials made from organisms, plant waste, and extracts, and sustainable processes becoming more advanced, the industry is going to see an entire upheaval at the start of the supply chain.

Inevitably some technologies will be adopted faster than others into the fashion industry. That's normal. However, what is clear is that tech is going to have a huge impact on the industry within the coming years and along with it new exciting ways of doing business. What is clear though is that it will take cross-industry collaboration for it to work and a global effort to bring all of the pieces together.

1.3. Definition of Fashion Tech

The ever-changing industry means that the term "fashion tech" will continue to evolve as new technologies are introduced. When defining it, we believe that it is the application of cutting-edge and innovative technologies as solutions to the fashion industry. In other words, the modernization of the industry to improve conventional ways of design and production, to customer experiences and everything in between.

Depending on which part of the value chain a brand may decide to integrate technology, "fashion tech" serves a purpose to each. While some consider AI for data analysis of fashion trends, others aim to immerse their customers into a digital version of the physical store in virtual reality. One thing in common with all of these is that the fashion brands and retailers usually need to outsource the expertise and solutions to make the "tech" in "fashion tech" possible. Key players then include tech startups, leaving room for impactful collaborations with brands to transform fashion.

Only within the last 10 to 15 years has fashion tech been taken seriously by the fashion industry, let alone other industries, and more mainstream cases have only just begun to be produced since 2020. From more digital fashion departments being introduced into fashion brands to more digital fashion garments introduced in gaming, we are just at the brink of fully convincing the industry leaders and trendsetters of the potential that technology has to bring. Resources, money, and different stakeholders (e.g., investors and tech geniuses) are required to move this forward in all parts of the value chain.

1.3.1. Front-End Technologies

Due to its broad nature, the definition and understanding of fashion tech are ambiguous to those in and out of the fashion industry. Those who work in fashion brands and retailers while staying up to date with fashion innovation news may be familiar with the emergence of particular innovations such as digital garments that have suddenly taken a place in fashion. This is an example of a front-end technology that is more visible or usable by the end customer. It's until one studies the possibilities of introducing technologies such as these to optimize the industry that the term "fashion tech" begins to make sense particularly when categorized as "front-end."

One of the main players who have shown interest in fashion tech are fashion designers. Many aspiring fashion designers, those who are upcoming and design garments and other fashion products at small scale, usually dream of having their own boutique. However, with the oversaturated world of the Internet and social media, it has never been harder to stand out. This is where we see the use of visually aesthetic innovations that help to push the designers in front of the faces of their customers in ways that other designers may not yet have explored. This is more than just a cool video on their website; nowadays, an example could be floating digital garments worn by hyper-real digital avatars and surrounded by curated virtual environments, and it is the new norm to showcase products. For established fashion brands, something like this is used more as a marketing tool to represent themselves as a brand that embraces tech while testing other various metrics such as customer engagement. This can also be in a physical store setting where the front-end technologies would augment the traditional experience of the customer shopping journey. These innovations will be explored further throughout the book.

Since the more established brands tend to already have the financial stability for these implementations, this leaves room for deeper developments and multiple heads that could combine and innovate further. Companies such as Skinvaders do exactly that – introducing fashion brands to the metaverse with their tech and gaming expertise that could heavily influence the marketing or usual way of retail for these fashion brands. We'll be talking about how fashion is entering the space later on in the book including Tommy Hilfiger's Tommy Factory campaign developed in partnership with Holition in Chapter 4.

To even further confuse what we have currently studied as "fashion tech," not all of it is simply left on-screen. Phygital is a term that represents the link between physical and digital realms. LVMH being one of the leading players doing this; one of their brands, Kenzo, has been offering digital versions of the physical garments, also known as "digital twins," that they sell on platforms, such as Decentraland. This allows customers to physically wear the garment as usual along with the digital asset that is the NFT version of the same garment. What is the point of it all? Well not only would you have physical products in this case but also digital assets that are a whole category in themselves and will be delved into much further in Chapter 2. These are just examples of how technologies have taken their place in the fashion industry with small brands as well as established ones from a very visual and customer-facing perspective.

1.3.2. Back-End Technologies

Other technologies that are not typically as aesthetic orientated, though, won't be as widely recognized as related to fashion such as AI, AR, blockchain, etc., but can be used on the back end. Now from the upstream phase of the value chain (everything before and including production), the uses of the technologies are more likely to be about the brand's desire for efficiency in areas of design, production, supply, and logistics, as opposed to "showing off" as we saw with front-end technologies. Here is where the traditional ways of working become irrelevant to create the products.

Back-end technologies are those that are implemented "behind the scenes," and customers may never even know about their existence from the surface, as it predominantly benefits the operations of the fashion business. From the point of view of the brand, whether small or established, their purpose is to do things differently and replace the exhaustive tasks that may not be as maintainable anyway for the long run when considering concerns such as sustainability. This includes machines such as Sewbot – an automation of the production of the garments, taking care of sewing garments that would usually be spread across multiple workers in a factory.

Such technologies use machine learning, which is a branch of AI for efficient results, where the computer is taught how to follow a certain algorithm to mirror human accuracy and gradually improve (IBM, 2023), while others still rely on human interaction throughout the processes. Having worked with students from IFA Paris, an international private fashion school, we are familiar with this from the side of the software that deals with everything before production, particularly involving pattern making from start to finish. These students have been exposed to pattern cutting software including Lectra's Modaris and N-hega's NShot Pro, allowing them to digitize existing paper patterns or make them digitally from scratch. Many benefits follow this, from quicker turnaround lead times to compatibility with other digital design software and the obvious avoidance of misplacements or physical damage that would usually risk with physical patterns. Sustainability is also indirectly contributed to with the options to lay plan the patterns and being able to efficiently plan the layout of the pattern to be cut in a way that reduces fabric waste.

Whether fashion students are introduced to these technologies at school, or they experience them when being implemented into established fashion brands that they will later work for, the same sacrifices are required to move these forward as per the front-end technologies. Time is still needed to learn the software and master it and the process that follows each software including translating an idea from design to digital pattern when working with the digital design software.

With these technological advancements comes also the knowledge that one needs to fully understand how to work with fashion tech in the differing areas, particularly the small brands who are likely to take on the work themselves compared to the established brands who have begun building additional departments that solely deal with these developments. This can be challenging for small brands that have limited resources or team members that are required to make the implementations possible internally. On one hand, time is taken to learn new software, master it, and then eventually create the final digital catwalk shows in immaculate quality as an example of the front-end technology. On the other hand, unless the brand happens to already have easy access to finances, usually fundraising may be needed to afford the expenses involved in working with an external tech company or consultant who can make the same digital show happen in just weeks. This can also be the difference between a brand choosing to work with lo-fi tech that is less complicated and already widely used such as online marketplace via websites or tills at the stores – typically easier and more straightforward to install or implement into the brand. The opposite would be hi-tech that is more complex regarding the expertise required to imbed it in the existing brand systems such as AI body scanners.

1.3.3. Fashion Tech Adoption

So what does this mean when defining "fashion tech" as a whole? We have seen that it is something that is applicable across the value chain with different purposes and various benefits as well as challenges. Despite this, we can see that the evolution has continued to spiral upward and multiply in different ways across the value chain.

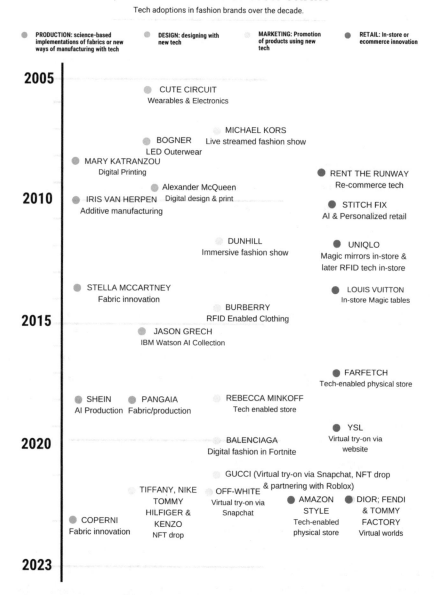

FASHION TECH ADOPTION CHART

Tech adoptions in fashion brands over the decade.

Figure 1-4. *Chart showing a snapshot of the earliest adoptions of tech by fashion brands just over the decade. Estimated from research conducted by Von and Peter.*

Figure 1-4 was created to visualize the adoption of technologies by some mainstream fashion brands across the last few years at different market levels. It is a zoomed-out lens on how fashion tech has grown and will be delved into more detail in each chapter. This chart considers the publicly announced partnering of the technologies discussed in this book with the brands after potential years of research or testing done prior and is a snapshot of what is happening in the industry. Some of the listed brands have tapped into multiple technologies, while others have experimented more privately. From our research, what has been publicly shared and the professionals we have spoken to through our work and the writing of this book, we can see that the whole supply chain can benefit from the adoption of technology even if certain areas may be doing so more rapidly than others.

A lot of information is not publicly available to refine the chart further; however, the research we have conducted reveals the popularity of the discussed technologies for retail and marketing advancements have been easier to adopt through plug-and-play methods. This makes the two areas the "technologically celebrated" areas more rapidly. You will see in Chapters 4 and 5 that these fashion tech efforts are to interact between the brand and the customer. From a technical standpoint, you will see that this is usually adding the tech on top of existing fashion brand systems and avoiding completely changing them.

While companies such as Shein have utilized AI-automated tech to drive fast fashion production linked to fashion trends from the back end, there is a relatively slower adoption of these kinds of production and design systems for other fashion brands. Ultimately, each fashion brand has the deciding power of which technologies work for them and their customers along with their values. For example, the end of 2021 and 2022 saw a rise in NFT releases by many luxury fashion brands beyond those listed in this chart due to the influence of the metaverse and value in traceability (as NFTs are linked to blockchain). According to Vogue Business (2021), "there is no fixed use or winning formula for brands";

therefore, it can often be a matter of keeping relevance when fashion brands adopt some of these technologies. An evolution of the customer's values will also help determine the technologies that will be further adopted and will be explored in the next section.

1.4. Fashion Tech Bingo

How would you define yourself? Are you on the tech side, fashion side looking for tech implementation, or a combination of these?Highlight the parts that apply to you and compare with which category you are working toward or need to collaborate with to innovate.

Table 1-1. *Fashion tech bingo activity*

Fashion brand/retailer	Tech startup/company	Fashion tech solution
Develops physical product (accessory, clothing, footwear, etc.)	Develops tech product or service (AI, AR, etc.)	Develops digital or fashion product/service
Identified niche/market level/competitors are selling similar fashion products	Focuses on tech results when testing market/ competitors are only tech focused	Tech teams and fashion teams collaborate (can be separate departments)
Aims for clients/consumers to purchase goods	Aims to help clients/ consumers to use tech product/services for more efficient or technologically advanced processes	Aims for clients/ consumers to purchase products of services in an unconventional way (product/service being the ultimate innovation as opposed to the process)

1.5. Defining the Market, Consumer, and User

The main stakeholders in all of the decisions for the direction of fashion tech are the consumers. The target market for all of this has almost automatically been calculated according to the brands that are adopting these technologies so far and on which platforms. The average person shopping in a store for garments may not want to spend their time and money on purchasing digital garments that cannot even be worn physically when concerning NFTs. On the other hand, those who have more disposable income (and time) are more likely to have the spending power to splash on other "not so essential things" such as these digital items worn by their digital twin (avatar version) in the metaverse or in computer games as skins.

Given this mixed message of exactly who is targeted here, it can be broken down into the distribution of population generations and their interests according to the brands and platforms that have so far tapped into fashion tech. Just like in any industry, fashion tech can be introduced to a customer at any generation to enjoy the fruits of the developments. In this case, the "fruits" are predominantly the front-end technologies that are easily measurable in terms of interaction between them and the customers. Understanding how the different individuals interact with fashion tech is how we can determine the current target market for it (whether on purpose or just by those who have adopted it naturally).

We can particularly observe the interaction between the B2C "fashion tech"–related products and the customers. Who is buying the Oculus Quest to take a shopping spree in the virtual stores via virtual reality? Who is buying their avatars a digital Balenciaga outfit on the virtual game Animal Crossing? Lastly, how much are they spending on these, or not?

Baby Boomers (1946–1964)

Probably known as the least likely to be interested in fashion tech, considering the emergence of tech in general having taken place at a later stage for them during their lifetime for both boomers and boomers II (also known as Generation Jones living as young kids through the 1960s). As previously mentioned, this is a general assumption that considers the value applied by the boomers to such innovations. Due to this, attitudes toward tech are more likely to be different to the other end of the generation distribution – Gen Alpha. Growing up with minimal to no personal computer technologies (besides kitchen appliances, etc.) impacts the initial reaction of this generation to technology in general. When comparing with other generations, impacts include the actual usage of the technologies not coming to them as natural as others (Statista, 2018).

When it comes to fashion tech, this is almost double the challenge especially when understanding the value of using it. For example, the need for a smartphone to communicate with others or the practical convenience of online shopping instead of going to a physical store is easier for them to understand the relevance. Now when it comes to purchasing an NFT? "You get to own a digital asset!" is more of a stretch as the value of this is not as clear without further research and explanation to the boomers. Any additional technologies that don't appear as a necessity are less likely to be adopted by this generation, resulting in them not being the primary target market for the front-end technologies mentioned.

Gen X (1965–1980)

Gen X are quite undefined when it concerns their interest in technology. They have had more exposure to it compared to Baby Boomers; however, they may still not see as much value as the later generations that will be explored in this section as previously mentioned. Considering the first introductions to teaching computing in schools emerged from the 1980s, it was still not widely practiced in all schools globally. This means there is half of the generation who may have had the introduction to other fashion technologies other than computers and smartphones during their workplace at another stage according to their professions. This makes Gen X a generation that can be identified as one that predominantly adopts fashion tech in an unpredictable cycle.

We have actually seen this in the workplace where some colleagues within this category attend additional courses to increase their general technological knowledge and further narrow it down to specifics such as digital marketing or digital fashion before taking it to the workplace. This not only shows a gap in the earlier education system between mandatory schooling, but also in further education where the later generations are able to access such fashion tech-related courses much younger than this generation. This also shows an interest of individuals in this generation to stay relevant to the surroundings for different purposes, including those needing to learn the related skills for a job or to have an additional entertainment in general. This can also be seen with half of the older millennials explored next.

Millennials (1981–1996)

They too are quite complex to analyze directly but for a different reason. They are the only generation to not have only witnessed but have also been immersed in the development of technology generally compared to Gen X (besides the older Gen Z's who also managed to see a glimpse of this tech revolution). They were not born with smartphones in their hands (as we usually consider the following generation to have done), which gives a different nuance on their skill set being based on learned behaviors as opposed to second nature at birth. While we don't mean this literally, this definitely has an impact on the attitudes where it is likely more mixed into this generation. While some will more easily accept the development of new technologies, the older Millennials may still not embrace fashion tech.

From the first launches of personal computers to all other technologies explored further in this book, Millennials are more likely to understand this more easily than the earlier generations but from two perspectives: (1) in a professional setting and (2) for home entertainment.

In professional settings:

Similarly to Gen X, introductions to general technologies are more likely during their career developments and definitely their profession. They would not be too unfamiliar when being introduced or trained to new technologies that are required at their workplace. Usually meaning they are a user of, for example, a digital design software as part of their 3D design role. This can apply for any other back-end technology that they need as part of their fashion tech job role.

For home entertainment:

Some will enjoy the virtual reality experience in the comfort of their own home as leisure, while others are comfortable to stick to the less complex front-end technologies in the forms of entertainment or online shopping on a smartphone that do not necessarily require training (which is more lo-fi tech that would have needed to be learned by this generation at some point, potentially during IT classes during early years of school).

To further confirm these two instances, a poll was done by Peter on Instagram (2022) where the majority of his followers are Millennials from different industries. There were significantly more votes voting "no" to the question of whether they had tested or at least heard of digital fashion before. "No" validates the point that further opportunities need to present themselves to encourage this generation to consider fashion technologies further.

Gen Z and Gen Alpha (1997–2012 and 2013–2024)

Now this brings us to Gen Z who are described as the "first digitally native generation" (Nokia & Ipsos, 2022). Considering their age group, Gen Z have a little more time on their hands than the typical Baby Boomers or Gen X's especially due to the stage of their lives that they are at. The main differentiation between this generation and the others is that Gen Z are more exposed to fashion tech directly, along with the younger Millennials. Filters readily available on TikTok, Instagram, and Snapchat are examples of the easy access to augmented reality without even knowing it and particularly of interest for Gen Z users. Fashion brands have partnered with social media platforms to directly showcase their products with technologies such as AR virtual try-on to directly access Gen Z who spend on average three hours on these platforms per day (Statista, 2022).

Gen Z, with Generation Alpha following just behind, are drawn to the metaverse and comfortable to spend on digital garments. The idea of having digital assets is considered the same value as purchasing the physical. What was once an average teenage boy's room filled with comics, sneakers, or caps is now an NFT wallet consisting of similar collections, only that it's all virtual. But why, you ask? Validation is the keyword here. For a generation that has grown up with Instagram and Twitter, it's the norm to want and accept validation online, even from strangers, for online content (Nokia & Ipsos, 2022). This is a clear difference between the attitudes across the generations according to their surroundings, what is pushed in schools, and timing.

Transferable skills obtained by this generation through the use of smartphones on a daily basis (from earlier ages than the other generations), to the general familiarity with the fact the technology is ever evolving, allow them to naturally and easily adapt to ever-emerging technologies. If we bring this back to the perspective of the brands and designers, they exploit the platforms that Gen Z and Generation Alpha use in order to sell products to them.

When looking into Gen Z at the IFA Paris private institution, we explored how this preexisting influence of technology could impact Gen Z fashion design students in their practices as the "next generation" of the fashion industry. A large group of students were studying Bachelor in Fashion Design, while the others were studying Master of Arts in Contemporary Fashion Design typically across ages of 18 to 25. Like other groups of students studying fashion-related courses, most of these students are currently not familiar with more tech other than what is being taught at the private institution. In this case, digital fashion design (which will be further discussed in Chapter 2) and basic science-based materials as per the results reflect in Figure 1-5a.

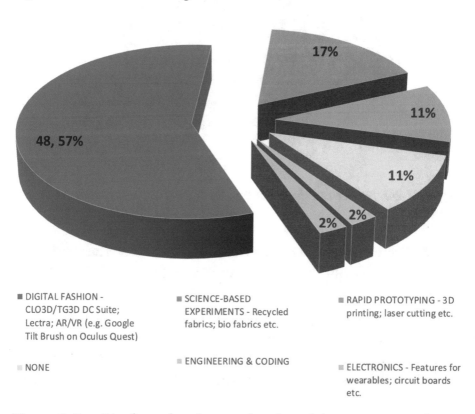

DIGITAL FASHION - CLO3D/TG3D DC Suite; Lectra; AR/VR (e.g. Google Tilt Brush on Oculus Quest)

SCIENCE-BASED EXPERIMENTS - Recycled fabrics; bio fabrics etc.

RAPID PROTOTYPING - 3D printing; laser cutting etc.

NONE

ENGINEERING & CODING

ELECTRONICS - Features for wearables; circuit boards etc.

Figure 1-5a. *Pie chart showing results of participant responses from IFA Paris*

Considering the competence of this generation in lo-fi tech, it is evident that there is still plenty of room to be nurtured in the world of more hi-tech fashion technologies including digital fashion software, science-based materials, etc., that we highlight as the more recently developed examples of fashion tech throughout this book. As shown in Figure 1-5b, 95% of the sampled students responded that they had never experienced any types of the technologies with brands (beyond the ones usually available at their fingertips through AR filters on social media, etc.), whether that is through internships, work, or generally as a customer.

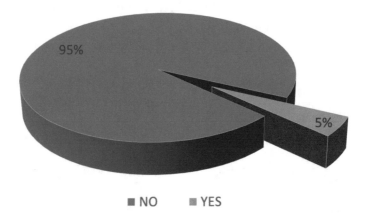

■ NO   ■ YES

Figure 1-5b. *Pie chart showing results of participant responses from IFA Paris*

All of the aforementioned mean that no generation can be pinpointed as "the" generation that has fully delved into fashion tech. Instead, we can define the target market for the back-end technologies as a group of individuals who are now working in the newly developed departments in fashion companies or interested in fashion for their leisure or augmented experiences with the front-end technologies. There is still a long way to go before it all becomes mainstream, where fashion tech would be widely used as part of every day at any part of interaction between customer and brand. This is why the CEO of IFA Paris Group, Jean-Baptiste Andreani, saw the importance of introducing fashion technologies such as digital design software to the students which Von has taught at IFA Paris. While these efforts are being positively received by students who wouldn't usually have their brains wired to consider tech in their pursuit of working in the fashion industry after graduation (Andreani, 2023), there are still barriers which Andreani has highlighted:

> *"When you deal with disciplines like upcycling, you can do it almost immediately but, when it comes to tech, there are many steps that you need to learn first. You need to learn, for example, to do 3D modeling before you can do any sort of 3D printing. You need to learn the basics of digital design before you start creating an NFT or building an experience in the Metaverse. There is also an element of marvel of this new technology, but there is also a barrier in terms of understanding and realizing in a concrete manner, what can tech bring to the plate?"* *(Andreani, 2023)*

In other words, fashion students still need convincing of the significance of the technologies that they are being introduced to. The future of the fashion tech space is partially in the hands of Gen Z who are currently experiencing what appears to be a "guinea pig phase" and paving the way for Generation Alpha who are soon to follow what comes from this period. As Gen Z are only now getting this introduction to digital fashion amidst the rest of what fashion tech has to offer with hi-tech, the next few years will unveil the next phase of "fashion tech" according to the new values that may be developed.

1.6. Chapter Summary

Fashion tech may appear to be difficult to define initially at a glance. It is just as difficult for some customers, depending on their generation, to wrap their heads around the purposes of some of the fashion technologies too. A mobile phone that was once recognized as just a means of communication is now a smartphone beyond its primary function with access to everything on the Internet, highly advanced apps, financial services, and maybe even haptics in the future. On just a smartphone alone (never mind other devices such as tablets and VR headsets), there are a wide variety of opportunities for fashion brands, whereby fashion tech can be accessed and utilized by many types of users from a professional and consumer perspective.

What we can learn from this chapter:

1. Fashion tech has the potential to touch every part of the fashion value chain. Some areas such as marketing and retail have been transformed more than others such as design.

2. The definition of fashion tech is broad, and it is down to the fashion brand to interpret what it means and its application to their business.

3. Millennials and younger generations will adopt fashion tech solutions a lot easier and quicker. However, newer technologies will still take time for all to adopt into their lives.

To make it easier to digest and understand where a brand could make sense of new technologies, it is required to understand where the major pain points and needs are first. Then we can work backward to understand where it can be applied throughout the value chain.

Activity for brands:

1. Map out the value chain for your business (like in Figures 1-1 and 1-3).

2. Identify where you have the biggest pain points and opportunities for fashion tech to be applied to (like in Section 1.2 and Figure 1-4). For example, you are currently only designing products by hand drawing, which does not give you a realistic view of what it could look like in physicality.

3. With the gaps identified, make a wish list of technologies that you believe could help you. We'll then see if any of the fashion tech discussed in this book matches and hopefully inspires you to take action.

CHAPTER 2

Next Evolution of Design

2.1. Can Anyone Now Become a Designer?

2.1.1. No-Code Designing

When having done something for so long, it becomes second nature; for fashion designers, drawing using pen (or pencil) to paper has always been the thing. Before the camera was introduced to the world, as we all know it, the talented painters and drawers were heavily relied on for illustrating what couldn't previously be captured. This is one of the reasons for the amazing fashion illustrations we see today. When we say this, we particularly reflect on the early Vogue magazine issues with pages filled with animated versions of garments and fashion collections. Fast-forward to the mid-2000s, computer-aided design (CAD) gets introduced, and suddenly we are all learning how to sketch with a mouse and screen. Moving forward again, we now see all sorts of unconventional ways to draw and show a fashion design idea.

From drawing 2D on Adobe Illustrator (as we learned) to now drawing in 3D on digital fashion software such as CLO3D. One thing that differentiates the two phases is the ability to apply technical pattern making knowledge for a final visual outcome when using 3D digital software. Needing to have experience in pattern making is vital for the final outcome. While usually a pretty garment is what is displayed at the end, the process of creating it is not so pretty. There is a need for accuracy in measurements and knowledge of what notches are; otherwise, digital clothing could easily be made back to front or with pockets in the wrong places.

Developers of such technologies, including tech startups, usually need to work with the pattern makers and seamstresses for this garment making knowledge, or the fashion brands must have this pattern making or sewing knowledge themselves or within a department. This is the only way a digital garment could come to life (or to digital life). If it were down to simply drawing a design in 2D as before, this knowledge would not be required for this part of the process (but would soon be needed to actually sew the physical garments).

Now when it comes to business, platforms that we have been working with like Drippy have taken it up a notch by exploiting the whole "design it yourself" approach, meaning even fashion beginners can now be designers. Drippy's 3D Builder platform means that those who aren't so gifted in the drawing or sketching department still can "design" garments (digital or physical). Digitally: the library of preexisting digital patterns allows the user to access options to either purchase for reuse on different platforms or to alter different design components on the 3D digital model. From changing sleeve lengths to changing the collar shapes, the "inexperienced" designer can create a final garment from each choice they make (Figures 2-1a, 2-1b, 2-1c). This instant visualization is what we have been working on with Drippy as the core feature matching the needs of industry that is usually fast and on demand.

Figure 2-1a. *Screenshot of Drippy's 3D Builder platform*

Figure 2-1b. *Screenshot of Drippy's 3D Builder platform*

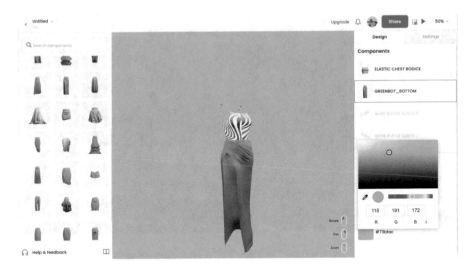

Figure 2-1c. *Screenshot of Drippy's 3D Builder platform*

Physically: the garments created from this could also be manufactured to become the physical version of themselves. With over 500 sign-ups within the beta testing phase, it is clear that platforms like Drippy are useful for those earlier-stage fashion brands or aspiring fashion designers to make their garments come to life in a less traditional way.

Earlier you may have noticed we said "design" in quotation marks as there are limitations to this aspect on such platforms. There is less emphasis on the designing element that is usually required for pen to paper or on other 2D digital software. This becomes more of a template-to-reality concept where the garments will be limited to the pre-set features, which makes this kind of platform unsuitable for the more seasoned designers/brands who specialize in designing from scratch.

This is where personalization comes in, where a tool like the 3D Builder can be exploited so that the customers too can use it for their own desired items. Handing the design power to the customer in this case, a customer can visit a brand website and access the different available design components that can allow them to select their overall design for their own purchases. While still presenting the 3D digital model as the look of their garment develops, the final design becomes an item that is owned by the consumer to later physically own. In this case, not only the designer is the "designer" as they would have needed to provide all of the templates for the sleeves, hems, etc., but the consumer too designs their ideal garment through combining the components as they desire. The business model then becomes more personalization based to cater to more needs of the customer than the usual online shopping. The freedom to create your own look helps to increase individuality. What that means for business is a group of customers more likely to be happy with their purchases as they are involved in the actual design process.

2.1.2. Generative Design: Are Computers the Designers?

So with all of this said, what really makes a designer? Is it the conventional fashion brands as we know it; the individual who has always wanted their own fashion brand so has used the 3D Builder to make it happen; or the consumer who has now more power to order their very own custom design through personalization tools? Well, this is something that can continue to be explored with the large options of tech in fashion now that generative design can be added to this list. Using artificial intelligence, digital designs can be created through a simple narration of instructions given verbally or via text. This could be classified as the computer or the tech being the designer as it pretty much does the hard work in the background; however, the human user would have the power to dictate their desired outcome. This ultimately makes them the decision maker in this process.

Tech startups like T-Fashion have begun to explore this. We have worked closely with T-Fashion initially through the Foundry Powered by IFA Paris incubator. They have developed their trend forecasting platform that gathers the trend data from various sources including Instagram to then allow AI to generate fashion trend insights and designs. As shown in Figures 2-2a, 2-2b and 2-2c, the process is easily broken down into these steps:

1.   Select a base item (in this case, a hoodie).

2.   Image of an example garment is uploaded: the hoodie.

3.   Type in the key prompts to determine the desired colors, print, fastening, etc. Prompts can look like "zip hood with black and yellow stripe pattern" as per Figure 2-2b or more detailed like in Figure 2-2c.

4.   Click "generate" for the design to be actualized.

Brands can save these images as a visual prototype to showcase on their online stores for customers to see the potential outcome of the physical garment that would be ordered. Its hyper-realistic visual quality allows an accurate depiction of the physical garment which one of the designers, Asher Levine in Figure 2-4d of the next section, has demonstrated. This can be a game changer for small brands where costs can be kept low by only manufacturing the garments once they have been instead of keeping large stock in inventory and hoping to sell them all.

Figure 2-2a. *Compilation of screenshots of T-Fashion trend forecast platform*

Figure 2-2b. *Screenshot of T-Fashion generative design platform*

Figure 2-2c. *Screenshot of T-Fashion generative design platform with more detailed prompt*

2.1.3. Hyperreality: 3D Digital Design

We've spoken about no skills required with the 3D Builder, personalization tools, and AI generative design, but the reality is that there are designers that still want an authentic design that is unique to their brand. Whether small or established brands, the role of the designer is still needed in the process; however, technologies can still transform the processes involved. It is no wonder why we are seeing new design departments and roles forming within brands such as the 3D digital designer, which we spoke about as one of the users for hi-tech fashion technologies in Chapter 1. Brands that are embracing digital assets and technologies like these include sportswear leaders, Nike, Under Armour, and Adidas, who we will explore in future chapters. 3D digital design is required to make this all happen. There are many 3D digital design software solutions that can be used to make these 3D digital garments, from CLO to Browzwear, that are more fashion focused compared to other 3D digital design software like Rhinoceros and Blender.

There is a difference between:

1. **Users of 3D digital design software** who have accepted the time required to still consider the digital pattern making processes for final outcomes as shown in Figure 2-3a. The sewing pattern is needed to simulate onto the 3D avatar to mirror the fit and balance of what the garment would be like in real life (also with the help of the fabric scanner in Figure 2-3b). If software pretty much forces users to design with the heavy reliance of pattern making and sewing knowledge, then the role of the designer would mean it requires pattern making knowledge in this case.

2. **Users of 2D digital design software** who would rather not think about patterns at all, focusing on the 2D visuals of the garments only. This could mean more people involved in this process including (a) the designer with all of the design ideas roughly illustrated on paper, (b) the pattern maker who interprets the design and creates the patterns for them, (c) the tech developer who translates the paper pattern to a digital one for simulation onto the 3D digital avatar, and (d) the manufacturer who sews the physical sample of the garment. This chain could continue on to NFT experts who mint the digital garments for digital assets and so on.

Figure 2-3a. *DC Suite by TG3D Studio showing the pattern making process on the left hand side of the screen and the 3D simulated outfit from the same pattern on the right hand side of the screen.*

Figure 2-3b. *Process of 3D digital software via DC Suite and fabric scanner by TG3D Studio*

What makes 3D digital design powerful is simply the hyperreal imagery that can be achieved. You'd think that humans prefer actual tangible items to marvel over; however, these digital designs almost look like they are jumping out from the screen, which provides a fascination that is unmatched. What could have been used as a marketing gimmick has actually been a new way to generate more revenue and save costs through converting these creations as commercial NFTs for instance, instead of distributing them for physical manufacturing in the traditional fashion world. The hyperreal designs are also realistic in the fact that patterns are required to make the garments behave on the body of the avatar as they would if sewn together in real-life fabric for a human body. This is also useful when focusing on the prototyping phase, where seeing the garment initially in this hyperreal way can help visualize it first before proceeding with the often costly physical sample. Whether the imagery is static or an animated catwalk with or without digital models, the technologies used still give an almost tactile look through the high-quality finishes including scanned fabrics and textures.

Does this mean technology has been advanced to deliberately mirror the conventional design processes required in real life (sketch to sample)? Or have these technologies taken certain parts of the real-life scenarios (in this case, pattern cutting) to transform the process for the same outcome just in digital form this time? What if the final outcomes were still possible to be achieved while avoiding certain technical knowledge needed (such as that needed for pattern making in both physical and digital design software)? This can be the future of 3D digital design software, to become easier for the implementations into brands. The challenge remains, for the workforce to be trained accordingly for this. The digital design process can be costly when concerning the training of the users from the design departments of the brands or when outsourcing the experts to complete all renderings.

Ultimately, the role of the designer continues to metamorphose along with the emergence of tech in fashion. We are convinced that it is down to the skills that you choose to utilize for your desired outcome. Whether this is the traditional drawing or sketching skills or if the strong point is pattern making or just building the tech itself.

2.2. The Role of Design in the Future
2.2.1. Designing Physical Products

Design languages are ever evolving, but as more fashion designers explore the possibilities of tech integrated into their design processes, the blueprint of fashion design is also changing. Moving away from the traditional 2D hand-drawn sketches where one dreams in silhouettes, seams, and fabrication, as discussed in the previous section, and ultimately shifting vocabulary to pixels, polygons, and code. Emerging fashion designers are increasingly becoming hybrid fashion, digital, and part tech experts. Previously it was about designing for the human body and artifacts that the body can adorn; fashion tech is allowing designers to think beyond the body but also the space around it. This could mean in the digital world where digital fashion includes animation and elements that don't even need to sit on the body, or in the physical world where objects can interact with the world around it by means of technologies such as IoT (Internet of Things). This is exciting and will ultimately push the creativity of design within fashion.

Designers such as Asher Levine are demonstrating the possibilities of new technologies in their design work and are blurring the boundaries between art, entertainment, fashion, and technology. Asher Levine is an emerging designer and label that started exploring technology with his fledgling brand in 2010 when singer Will.I.Am from the Black Eyed Peas approached him to create a light-up outfit to attend the Queen Elizabeth II Diamond Jubilee event. This served as the catalyst for tech exploration: *"I like to jump into unknown challenges. That's actually where innovation thrives"* (Levine, 2022).

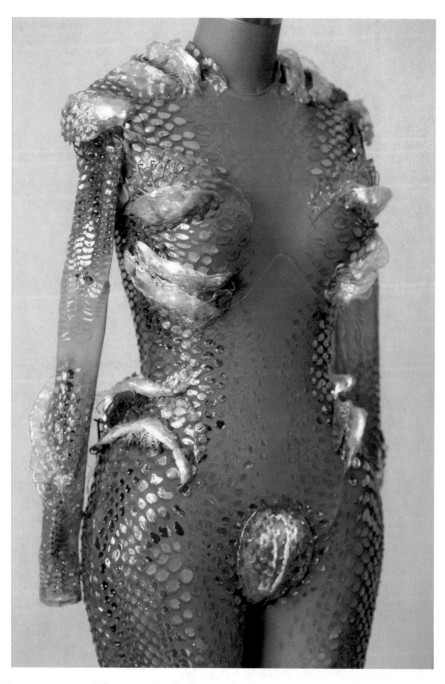

Figure 2-4a. *Asher Levine light-up bodysuit for singer Doja Cat*

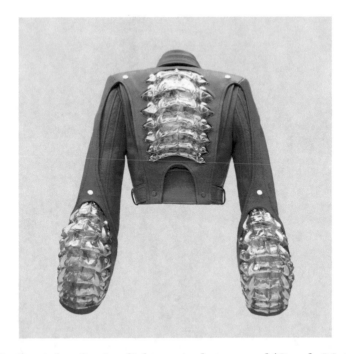

Figure 2-4b. *Asher Levine light-up jacket named 'Candy Moto'*

Figure 2-4c. *Asher Levine light-up jacket*

Figure 2-4d. *Asher Levine generative AI design work*

We interviewed Asher to delve deeper into how he has embraced
tech into his design process, in what he calls "*expressive illumination*"
(as shown in Figures 2-4a, 2-4b, 2-4c) and what he believes the role of the
design is in the future. For Levine, innovation in design means combining
techniques and materials not traditionally used in fashion such as
electronics, molded biomaterials, and rapid prototyping techniques. In
his design studio, there is a fashion department, a sculpture department,
and a tech department. For him, the role of the fashion designer is to
orchestrate and integrate all the complex and somewhat disassociated
pieces together. Does this then mean that the role of design is more
about context, relationships, social constructs, and how all of these are
interwoven?

For many designers, the notion of fashion tech commences with the physical product, which correlates to the way that fashion schools teach design, as mentioned in Chapter 1, but moving on from the physical is the digital. Levine is an example of a "traditionally trained tailor" that is now exploring the digital. *"I want my physical things to look like they're digital and I want my digital things to look like they're physical [Figure 2-4d)]. That is where I feel the opportunities and challenges are for design"* (Levine, 2022). He explains that fashion in the future will have the addition of digital layers, and this is what really excites him to push further into the space. Therefore, fashion design in the future is not just about thinking around the physicality but must also encompass the product's digital ecosystem surrounding it. The industry is already seeing the emergence of such projects with digital twins, digital IDs, and augmented reality (AR). We will explore this later in the book.

So what does this lead to? According to Levine, *"now is a time where we will see the individual expression enter a whole new area that we haven't seen before. I think we're going to move into a whole new world where the variety of shape expression will be at an all-time high saturation. I see the future becoming supersaturated with AI, sensors, IoT & Biometrics, and modern distribution is going to blur the boundary between raw material & the final consumer, and the idea of a brand will be diluted"* (Levine, 2022).

Levine expressed that designers wishing to enter fashion tech must reflect on the market opportunities based not on the short term or immediate now, but on the longer-term time horizon of between five and ten years. This notion does support the fact as to why there are not more designers pushing the boundaries with fashion tech, and an element of that is what Levine expressed as the unknown. For many fashion professionals, the unknown can be scary. As the survey concluded in Chapter 1, many new designers do not gravitate toward integrating technology into their practices naturally. Levine believes that this is because many designers do not have the desire to or fear embracing new tools. Therefore, what can be concluded is that more opportunities are needed to allow designers to get comfortable with fashion tech, whether this be within academia or the workplace. By doing so, the role of design will naturally evolve in the future, in which the creative process can be more innovative than it is now.

2.2.2. Fashion Design: Beyond Physical Products

Fashion design is usually synonymous with the notion of creating physical products, and the role of the designer is normally envisioned to be taking a drawing into a physical prototype. Digital fashion inverses this design paradigm, with many physical brands exploring digital versions of their physical collections or creating digital-only collections. This pushes the designer to think beyond the physical product because digital products offer a whole new world of use cases. This can mean computer games, virtual worlds, entertainment, and new forms of ownership. We'll explore each of these use cases later on in the book. These new opportunities allow designers to think about how customers will want to experience and consume their designs in the future beyond just owning the physical product.

Satoshi Studio is an example of a physical product brand selling sneakers that led its founder, Nicolas Romero, to create the digital sneaker NFT platform: Futures Factory. Romero, having been inspired by crypto banks and early NFT projects like CryptoKitties, saw an opportunity with the technology for sneakerheads (the term used to describe collectors of sneakers) having a potential positive impact on the way they will own, exchange, and collect items. He believes that such technology will allow brands to reinvent their business models, and for him, he is now thinking beyond the physical sneakers that he is selling. We spoke to Nicolas to unpack what fashion beyond physical products and NFTs means for fashion.

Futures Factory is a platform that helps footwear designers and brands to create their NFT projects, whether it's virtual only or backed by physical sneakers. Initially, Romero launched his line of sneakers with just €3000 on a pre-order and crowdfunding model but soon realized a stronger proposition to be had from a designer's perspective when he saw that customers were also buying digital art on NFT platforms such as OpenSea. He connected this with digital fashion designers: *"we knew that for them [the designers] concept sneakers were not meant to be physically made... so, they were totally unleashed on their creativity. No physical constraints"* (Romero, 2022). Figures 2-5a and 2-5b show the end results of how the digital sneakers are realized visually.

Figure 2-5a. *Futures Factory digital sneaker*

Figure 2-5b. *Futures Factory digital sneakers realized on an avatar*

Figure 2-5c. *Futures Factory avatar in motion*

Figure 2-5d. *Futures Factory NFT collection: Pioneers*

At the time of writing this book, Futures Factory has 12 team members, of which only one person comes from a fashion design background, their 3D footwear designer, whose role is to ensure that the digital fashion assets launched on the platform are usable in augmented reality or video games. The rest of the team is split between marketing, creative, and tech, which is indicative of the type of skills to get a fashion tech idea off the ground. For fashion designers looking to enter the fashion tech space, it highlights a secondary skill set needed to confidently converse with teammates. Romero advises designers to join digital fashion communities on Discord, a social platform allowing communities and their members to talk to each other, to get direct feedback and knowledge as to what potential users and buyers may be looking for. This test and learn cycle is quite different to what most fashion designers are used to, whereby a collection is designed and developed first before showing any potential customers. This model is what makes the traditional fashion collection seasons of spring/summer and autumn/winter. In this instance, we are talking between 6 and 12 months before feedback is gathered as opposed to almost instantly on Discord. Romero (2022) notes for the development of his own platform:

"They [the digital fashion enthusiasts] were super hard to convert into consumers. We realized that the people purchasing virtual sneakers were coming from the crypto world, so we had to change a lot of things in our [business] strategy and [product] offer to please them. I think the mainstream consumers will come with phygital sneakers. So, with the physical component, it will come later because right now we don't have all the big brands doing phygitals."

As Romero suggests, it will be the larger brands to lead the way for digital fashion mass adoption. The major players in 2022 consisted of Nike, Dolce & Gabbana, Tiffany, Gucci, and Adidas who topped the leaderboard for generating the most revenue from NFTs according to data by Dune Analytics (2022) across the NFT market. Nike had generated over $185 million by the end of 2022, which demonstrates that acquiring digital fashion platform RTFKT in 2021 has had a positive impact on their Web3 strategy. Romero recognizes the potential of fashion NFTs, which he is continually pushing new collections out to his community as shown in Figures 2-5c and 2-5d, the "Pioneers" collection.

For Futures Factory, this presents a design opportunity for fashion designers: *"the goal is to build the tools for brands and designers to create their projects in total autonomy and to back them with finance, the tech infrastructure and the community"* (Romero, 2022). This mindset induces cross-industry collaborations, most notably the gaming industry, which is seeing brands such as Burberry and Ralph Lauren entering the category in partnership with established gaming titles such as Minecraft and Fortnite. Other brands such as Tommy Hilfiger are combining several elements into multi-pronged campaigns such as their Tommy Factory campaign in September 2022 that live streamed digital fashion in Roblox and used NFTs as a proof-of-attendance protocol (POAP) to their physical event. In this instance, the products are used as content and means of entertainment. We'll talk more about the Tommy Factory campaign in Chapter 4.

2.2.3. Insider Perspective: What Fashion Designers Need to Learn for Competitive Advantage. Interview with John Lau, Dean of Academic Strategy at London College of Fashion

John Lau was previously the Associate Dean of the School of Design and Technology at LCF before becoming the Dean of Academic Strategy. As a trained fashion designer and with experience across multiple functions within fashion, he has a unique inside perspective of where the industry has been and where it is now heading. He and his team ensure that the academic programs at LCF are in sync with industry evolution. Peter sat down with him to discuss what designers need to know to be successful in the industry.

PJHT: How did you get into the fashion industry?

JL: I was a student at LCF where I graduated in womenswear design that led me to my first entry into the industry. From there, I realized that there was so much more in the industry to learn and understand so I moved into fashion magazines. From magazines, I then moved into production, which I just fell in love with, being able to work on complex business issues. This led me to study a master's degree in Business Enterprise.

PJHT: What did it do for you professionally moving from design to business?

JL: I think it made me understand the design process better, the stakeholders involved, and why the process is sometimes fixed in a certain way. A lot of the times when I see students conduct research is that they're researching without a specific purpose in mind. This applies to innovation as well, because how do you know what you're looking for? Accidents of course do happen, but these are very rare, and my business degree really helped me to understand how to find purpose.

PJHT: How does LCF define fashion tech?

JL: They're tools in the designer's toolbox. I say *tool*s for a very specific reason as they aren't there to replace analog design, but to enhance it. Of course, pen to paper is still very important for the design process, and you need to understand that before you can move onto tech tools.

PJHT: What tools are you referring to?

JL: 3D printing, rapid prototyping, but the biggest development in recent years has been 3D modeling to create digital fashion and using technologies such as Optitex, Gerber, Lectra, and CLO3D. These have nurtured the students' perspectives; they can design much faster, cleaner, and more sustainably than they have ever done before. The design process has shortened because designers can visualize the output quickly, correct mistakes, but also enhance the design based on what's presented to them digitally.

PJHT: What skills should designers acquire to ensure future employability and desirability?

JL: Traditional hand design skills should also include digital. What they really need is the ability to be able to situate their concepts in the physical world and digital spaces. Even though you may end up with a physical product at the end, the technology that we have means that we can design without making but still see hyper-realistic details up close. It takes skill to do that.

PJHT: What are brands looking for when they approach LCF to recruit graduates?

JL: They're looking for specialisms, and companies are not just looking for a "fashion designer." They're looking for specific skills and competent tech operators across a variety of hardware and software. At LCF, we have the whole ecosystem of fashion, which we mimic the job roles that are in demand within the industry.

PJHT: You've just launched an MSc in Fashion Analytics and Forecasting? Tell me why you decided to launch an atypical program.

JL: Fashion generates a lot of data: sales, production, and PDM (product data management) systems. Data can help the [fashion] system to be much more sustainable, help us make better design choices, and make long-term forecasting decisions. A lot of the fashion industry is still a guessing game; we guess what the audience wants, what the consumers want, but what data can tell us are trends and demands with accuracy. The program is training data analysts for fashion brands. These students are using data to build knowledge and the ability to undertake critical analysis to make better business decisions. We're seeing an oversubscription for the program, enough for two cohorts each year, and the industry will see more fashion tech roles like this come to the forefront.

PJHT: Where do you think the industry is heading then with fashion tech innovation?

JL: Every area in fashion will be impacted. It's about automating systems and people understanding the information that's being presented to them. I think that's been so important for the fashion industry since in the past this information was available to them, but they didn't know how to use it, or they didn't understand where it should be integrated in the value chain. Now there is a much clearer idea. I call this industry adjacencies because a lot of the tech that we are using is from other industries not necessarily related to fashion. We might be using it in architecture, for example, or in engineering, and it's transferring that into fashion design and context; that's what's interesting to me.

PJHT: From an educational perspective, do you think that we're going to be seeing more of those adjacencies?

JL: Absolutely, yes!

2.2.4. Future Design Workforce

There are approximately 3500 fashion design graduates per year showcased at Graduate Fashion Week in the UK (Graduate Fashion Week, 2022); this is a fraction of the number of graduates globally. It's no secret that fashion is incredibly difficult to break into for designers and creatives; therefore, beyond the traditional skills taught at fashion schools, most designers will need to up their game with the current demands of the fashion brands. This could mean additional capabilities such as digital fashion skills on software that we've already explored in this chapter or incorporating a more data-driven approach to design by utilizing analytical platforms such as T-Fashion (discussed in Section 2.1), Edited, or StyleSage to inform their design output.

According to the U.S. Bureau of Labor Statistics (2022) Employment Projections program, the number of fashion design jobs in the U.S. is projected to grow 3% between 2021 and 2031. This is below the 5% average for other types of occupations, meaning that there are all these fully trained designers, but simply not enough jobs to go round. Our own personal experiences certainly have shown us that many of our university course colleagues from fashion design have left the industry to go onto opportunities with more employment and career progression potential. (Peter would say that more than 50% from both his undergraduate and postgraduate degrees.) Ironically, many of the founders that are creating digital fashion and product development platforms that we've worked with inside the incubator come from outside of the fashion industry. Although not formally trained in fashion, what the founders do bring are technological and commercial sensibilities that bring a different dimension to design and product development.

"Fashion designers in the future won't just be sewing, they'll be coding" believes supermodel Karlie Kloss (Kloss, 2022). This belief is backed up by her free coding program "Kode With Klossy" that provides young women and nonbinary individuals between the ages of 13–18 with learning experiences to boost their confidence with coding. Kloss illustrated this further in 2022 with her first foray into the metaverse for her collaboration with Roblox entitled "Fashion Klossette Designer Showcase" as shown in Figure 2-6. She invited digital fashion designers to create and showcase their designs at the digital fashion pop-up, which garnered two million unique players in two weeks. This notion of community innovation is what's going to be driving how fashion design departments are going to be shaped in the future.

Figure 2-6. *Fashion Klossette Designer Showcase*

For the fashion designer, the need to be multifaceted is necessary to have a competitive advantage to maintain desirability in the industry. This means anything from understanding how their products will sell across all digital and physical touch points by utilizing technology and data (and thus data-driven merchants) or being technically able to evolve the traditional design process, such as being able to technically design trims using 3D software, creating them on rapid prototyping machines, and effectively communicating all of that to a nontraditional factory (and thus tech-driven futurists). For anyone looking to get into the design or product development side of fashion, we recommend building a skill set stack, as shown in Table 2-1.

Table 2-1. *Skill set stack checklist*

	Skill set stack		
	Base	**Gives an edge**	**Advantageous**
Stack 1: Traditional design	Skills that are taught in fashion schools: hand drawing, flats, pattern cutting, product construction etc.	Digital manipulation (think Mary Katranzou) and rapid prototyping (3D Printing, laser cutting etc.) Understanding of next generation materials (bio fabrics etc.)	3D design (Clo3D, Browzwear, Marvellous Designer etc.) Digital PLM (Lectra, Gerber etc.)
Stack 2: Tech enabled design	Knowledge using analytical and management platforms like Edited.com, T-Fashion etc. Ability to design in VR.	Ability to use data to back designs. Ability to transfer designs into different mediums, e.g., metaverse, AR filters.	Ability to implement design feedback loops to further collections- E.g., blockchain, digital passports etc. Ability to use non-fashion-related tech in design process.
Stack 3: Fully technical design	Creative coding. Understanding of hardware integration (Raspberry Pi, electronics etc.)	Ability to implement tech-led processes. E.g., Scrums, product management etc. Ability to implement UI/UX into design process.	Understanding of front and back-end systems to design & build products.

Side note: The term "stack" is normally used in the tech industry to describe the combination of technologies a company uses to build and run an application or project. For example, a "Full Stack Developer" is a job role for an individual that understands both back- and front-end technologies. When discussing the future of the fashion designer, a similar principle can be applied since both job functions are about needing specific technical skills to get a project, or in this case, a collection to completion for the market. As we can see in stack 3 in the table, this would be an individual fully immersed in the world of fashion tech who ultimately should be thinking about acquiring a "full stack" skill set.

Although it may seem like a tall order for a fashion designer to develop additional technical skills not traditionally associated with the role, according to FTAlliance's research (2022), the top eight roles within fashion tech in the future will be

1. Innovation Manager

2. UX Designer

3. Digital Experience Manager

4. Sustainability Lead

5. Digital Product Manager

6. Data Scientist

7. Lobbyist

8. Micro-factory Manager

Upskilling design teams with in-demand skills is a must, we feel, to maintain competitive advantage, either as an individual or as an organization. Peter's former students on the MBA Fashion Technology program at IFA Paris once asked why there was such an emphasis on modules such as data science and coding. The answer was simple: to be articulate in the tools, concepts, and language that many of the brands will demand and individual professionals will possess in the future. Nonetheless, it's not to say that designers have to be exceptional coders but rather are confident enough to have conversations that concern tech as the industry technically transforms.

2.3. Chapter Summary

The notion of fashion design is evolving to be more than creativity and pen to paper. Although still an important aspect, innovation in design must also involve technology to take it further. By utilizing tools such as 3D design, the boundaries of creativity can be pushed further, while utilizing technology such as generative AI can help ground design decisions in data and objectivity.

What we can learn from this chapter:

1. The fashion design process is evolving with tools such as no-design-skill-required applications, generative design, and more. Individuals from nondesign backgrounds can create fashion and may even think in a different design language such as pixels and polygons.

2. Fashion designers and developers would be best placed to acquire skills beyond traditional fashion design processes, thus becoming more desirable talent for fashion brands.

3. Digital fashion is an important part of the fashion design and development process. Brands no longer need to have physicality to be able to create collections.

Activity: Create and wear your own digital garment.

Table 2-2: Here is a list of things to try and see hyperreal digital fashion in action. This will also help give further context for the following sections and later chapters to understand the final stages of digital fashion including NFTs, digital fashion marketplaces, virtual try-ons, and digital fashion shows. To access links, use the QR code from the beginning of the book.

Table 2-2. *Digital fashion activity checklist*

App/software	To try	Check?
Check out Digital Fashion Weeks	See how digital fashion designers and fashion brands are creating 3D assets	
Watch the Gary James McQueen digital fashion film	See the different ways to showcase digital garments	
SWOP	Design a digital fashion garment using AI	
OuttaWRLD	Create and customize a digital garment in AR	
The Fabricant	Co-create and mint a digital fashion asset	

CHAPTER 3

Production and the Connected Supply Chain

3.1. Next-Generation Materials

Factories of the future, what will they look like? Fashion production still relies mainly on cheap manual labor to produce the 100 to 150 billion garments per year (Fashion United, 2023) compared to other verticals such as automobile and transportation. As discussed in Chapter 1, the Fifth Industrial Revolution is upon us whereby man and machine will have a more symbiotic relationship to automate tasks and achieve greater efficiencies. Boundaries are being pushed in the fields of science with R&D activities such as biomaterials, and technology is enabling the once-opaque fashion supply chain to be more accessible – accessible in terms of anyone now with a computer and Internet connection can source suppliers using user-friendly online platforms and manufacture garments in small quantities on demand at a click of a button. This connectedness in the supply chain will further increase manufacturing capabilities for brands small and large and facilitate globalization and localization at

© Von N. Ruzive and Peter Jeun Ho Tsang 2023
V. N. Ruzive and P. Jeun Ho Tsang, *Fashion Tech Applied*,
https://doi.org/10.1007/978-1-4842-9694-3_3

scales yet to be seen. This presents advantages such as allowing more variety of products to come to the market, thus lowering market entry barriers, but can also exacerbate issues such as overproduction.

Raw fibers and materials, the basis of all physical products and the start of the supply chain, present many opportunities for material sciences to flourish (literally when it comes to bio fabrication) with the advancement of hard technologies. Pangaia and Allbirds are examples of fashion brands that have fabric innovation baked into their company DNA. Pangaia with their Pangaia Lab has launched products with materials made from raw fibers such as fruits, wildflowers, alternative plants such as nettle, brewed protein, and regenerated waste. In the same vein, Allbirds' success stems from the way they use materials to develop their footwear lines with raw fibers derived from sugars and trees. The dawn of next-generation materials is a shift into more sustainable consumption, and although many next-gen materials are yet to be at the fully commercial stage, exciting things are expected to launch onto the market within the next ten years.

We previously partnered with AltMat, a great example of a startup fabricating material innovation, at the Circular Fashion Summit (we'll talk more about Lablaco, the company behind the summit in Chapter 4) to showcase the possibilities of how agricultural waste could be turned into beautiful fashion fabrics. The founder, Shikha Shah, describes AltMat as a house of alternative materials with a vision to build a supply chain infrastructure for turning waste into textile fibers. "*If you see agriculture waste, the simple question then is that if there's enough food globally, there's even more waste for the world*" (Shah, 2022). Shah's goal is turning the abundant waste into usable fabrics applicable for fashion as well as other verticals, making a positive impact in production. However, this requires significant hard tech advancements to achieve commercial scalability.

For many startups like AltMat, the starting point is investigating a problem from a scientific perspective and then layering technology on top to test the feasibility. In the case of AltMat, Shah realized that agricultural waste is lignocellulosic and that many textiles are cellulosic, meaning that the DNA of the elements is similar and proving that waste is a suitable input for textile manufacturing. The magic happens inside a biorefinery with AltMat's proprietary technology that utilizes a 14-step process consisting of a combination of mechanical, chemical, and microbial methods that upcycles the fibrous waste into softer, dye pickable, and spinnable fibers (highlighted in Figure 3-1a). The result is a cotton-like structure (Figure 3-1b) ready for turning into yarns and then eventually finished fabrics and garments (Figure 3-1c).

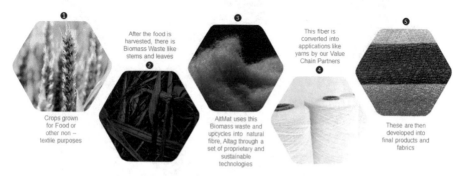

Figure 3-1a. *AltMat process of turning waste into fabric*

Figure 3-1b. *Spun AltMat finished fibers into yarns*

Figure 3-1c. *Garments made from AltMat fabrics*

Many material innovations such as AltMat's require lengthy lead times to get them from pilot stage to commercial scale ready, up to ten years depending on the complexity of the material, but AltMat has managed to cut this lead time in half through rapid iteration. Shah explains that for her to scale AltMat, her process is to look at the innovation progress from two angles:

- Phase 1: Inward looking. What are the results of the tests and pilots, and how can they be improved? The first AltMat biorefinery handled up to 200 kg of waste per day, which has subsequently scaled to 3 tonnes per day. At present, for every tonne of pure fiber produced, the process requires approximately between 1.2 and 1.35 tonnes of waste feed.

- Phase 2: Outward looking. Which brands can commit to production scale and have the consumption volume? If we take the numbers from phase 1, this produces between four and five million garments per day. For Shah, this is at a small scale, and her goal is to scale this up to ×10 by 2028.

Technicalities and sustainability aside, what is interesting is how Shah as a founder is mindfully building the foundations of the business with economic and inclusivity models also integrated (Figure 3-1d). Therefore, for a new material innovation to self-sufficiently thrive in the market and to coexist with traditional fabrics, it needs all these elements.

> *"What excites me is rearranging the supply chain to make sure that the new age biomaterials and innovations do not come at the cost of inclusivity...it can only happen if it also makes economic sense. I feel that we [the industry] also forget that fact as much as it is a question of environmental sustainability."* (Shah, 2022)

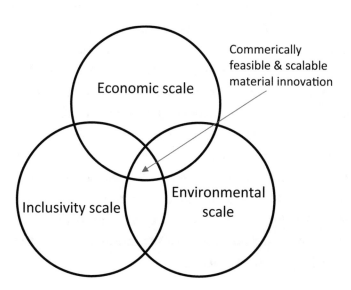

Figure 3-1d. *Diagram showing what next-gen materials require to scale*

3.2. Sourcing

Historically, for a fashion brand as a new entrant in the market, it was difficult to find the right suppliers and source the materials that matched the product vision. We've both been there having started our own independent fashion lines; to figure out where and who to go to first was a conundrum. However, with online marketplaces now extremely advanced and breaking down global barriers, companies like SwatchOn, Material Exchange, and Nona Source make it easy for designers and brands to obtain samples as well as yardage for bulk production catering to all market levels. Interestingly, Nona Source is the result of an intrapreneurial (the process of executing a startup or entrepreneurial project within an existing company) project born out of the French luxury conglomerate, LVMH Moët Hennessy Louis Vuitton (LVMH for short), to revalue their deadstock fabrics and make available to external third parties. This shows that the industry is becoming more open to sharing (just a little) due to digital transformation.

Companies like AltMat are developing next-generation materials that are game changers, but this also means adding a layer of complexity to understanding what these fabrics do and their potential impact on product development, manufacturing, and the environment. We need more than just marketplaces, and technologies for sourcing and managing fabrics are becoming more sophisticated. Queen of Raw (Figure 3-2) started life as a marketplace for deadstock fabrics serving the buy side but has evolved their solution to become a suite of "modules" that allow a company to manage their excess inventory in the cloud. The software named "Materia MX" allows the brand to understand whether they can reuse, recycle, or resell their excess stock and what this may mean from an environmental, social, and corporate governance (ESG) perspective. Founder Stephanie Benedetto realized more was needed:

"When we started, we were just seeing the marketplace for resale and what we learned is that for large enterprise companies to be able to participate in resale solutions they needed something that could scale. So that's how we evolved into Materia MX, a full stack software solution that provides clients with producing quick and easy reports in a private portal to measure elements required for their ESG reporting." (Benedetto, 2023)

The evolution of Queen of Raw into Materia MX has helped Benedetto acquire Fortune 500 companies globally as clients, in which fashion brands are successfully able to utilize their platforms for their ESG agendas. Ralph Lauren from using the software managed to see:

- 92% of waste diverted from landfill and incineration.

- 11.8 metric tonnes of unused materials rescued.

- Two key sourcing countries covered successfully, China and Vietnam, and expanding to other countries in 2024.

For Queen of Raw, another fashion client reduced their material waste and costs while growing sales and reaching new customers to achieve a return on investment in year one of working together. Not only was there a positive response, but by virtue of marketing the work with deadstock, the brand saw a ×3 conversation rate in the online direct-to-consumer business as a result of the campaign (Benedetto, 2022). For us, this is where investing in new fashion tech innovations is more than just R&D and has a direct impact on the core business. From an environmental perspective, collectively Queen of Raw has saved $1B+ gallons of water to date, which is enough clean water for 1.4 million people to drink around the world for three years.

Figure 3-2. *Queen of Raw at the Cartier Women's Initiative*

3.3. The Making

In Chapter 2, we spoke about the need for pattern making skills even just to design digital garments on software. When focusing on prototyping, it is just as important to get the desired physical garment; however, as the research with students has shown, pattern making isn't the most desired role. While more generations of fashion designers are being pumped out of schools and programs, not as many individuals are interested in pursuing the technical parts of creating the 2D patterns afterward. 2D patterns are flat shapes that are typically drafted or printed on paper that later on become the templates for the physical garments when cut onto fabric and sewn together so that the final design can be created. As a small brand owner like Von, one usually has to take on multiple roles including pattern making before or during the design phase. Typically, the pattern making part of production is not as creative as the visual designing part on other non-pattern-needed soft tech, which makes this part of the design process heavier. This leaves more room for alternative methods to get the pattern making job done. One way that many small brands have done this is to completely avoid this part by simply allowing their manufacturers to do this from designs they have illustrated or photos. Neither way is going to always provide 100% accuracy, meaning pattern making isn't always able to be avoided (even by the manufacturers of the brands as opposed to the brands themselves). You may see where we are heading with this.

That's right, technology is one of the forces that could completely change this part of the fashion supply chain. There are many ways this could happen. Lectra is one of the companies helping brands to digitize patterns or making them from scratch digitally using their software, Modaris. Having worked with large brands such as Calzedonia, the technology has been created for scans to remain life size on the software while being able to zoom into every inch of detail when editing with features to speed up the process. There is the ability to export these patterns as templates for use in other 3D digital software to dress a 3D digital avatar mentioned in Chapter 2, while the patterns could also be physically printed later for physical sampling.

Time can be saved during these sampling processes as the digital patterns are made to be easier and faster to detect any pattern issues or sewing issues that may arise in real life, eradicating the often-lengthy manual examining of issues in real life. Translating this flat digital pattern into a 3D digital avatar produces instant results of whether it works or not as a garment sewn together, vs. having to physically sew the samples of these patterns and then trying them on a real-life model. The digital aspect almost cuts out this whole manual and often tiring process, especially when having to compare multiple patterns together when sampling.

We can also look at N-hega who is a leading pattern digitizing company who has worked with many brands for similar purposes using their expertise in automatic scanning and AI. In this case, their N-Shot Pro pattern digitizer helps to digitize patterns by scanning them with the help of the precisely positioned camera overlooking the wide greenscreen table connected to the software. This digitization of the pattern allows you to extract it digitally and is editable. Being able to straighten lines and build on this existing pattern digitally, similar to Modaris, helps to create finalized patterns quickly. In the end, you will have a digital pattern that is:

1. Ready to send electronically to manufacturers for production.

2. Eligible to be exported to be compatible with Lectra or other software for further editing.

3. Ready to be printed in life size to create a physical sample of the garment.

All of the aforementioned will have an impact on other challenges in fashion such as sustainability. Many people in the industry often throw that word around, but in this case, the emphasis is more on how the brand can practice more sustainable activity, specifically the amount of fabric being saved during the process. Waste in the fashion industry has a lot to do with the early production processes too, particularly the fabrics. Often customers or those not knowledgeable about the production systems in the industry may consider "waste" as just unsold goods in the retail phase later on down the line; however, a minimum of 15% of fabric is usually lost as offcuts earlier on in the supply chain (Langenheim, 2022).

Simply cutting the patterns on the fabrics efficiently is an answer to this waste problem, also known as "lay planning" – patterns being arranged accordingly for the most efficient use of the fabrics. Think of it as a Tetris game with patterns instead of blocks. It can often be difficult to cut a pattern with this in mind on a fabric due to the positioning needing to be accurate as shown in Figure 3-3a. There is also something called the "grain line," which is usually printed on the pattern as a guideline to how the pattern must be laid in parallel to the edge of the fabric (also known as the selvage) to allow the fabric to behave accordingly when it has been made into a garment further down the line. Manually balancing between this grain line and saving as much fabric as possible from the cutting process can be overwhelming and often time consuming; some may even argue that it takes longer than the sewing itself. This is the reason for AI aiding in this part of the process through N-hega's NEstimate-Auto software (Figure 3-3b).

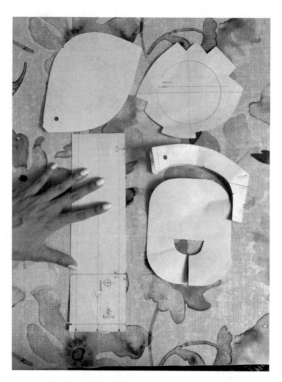

Figure 3-3a. *Manually moving around the sewing pattern on fabric according to the grain line*

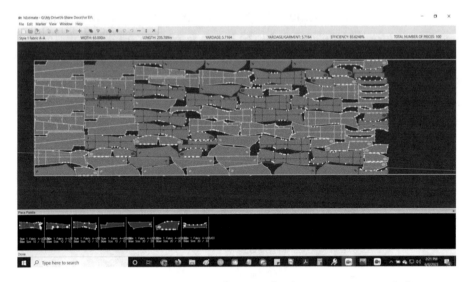

Figure 3-3b. *NEstimate-Auto software during an automatic lay-planning process*

Benefits of this technology:

- The software takes just two minutes to create a marker and estimate the fabric consumption, whereas a person manually creating this marker can take several minutes to hours to achieve the same result, depending on their experience.

- Lower labor costs by using less time to manually align patterns.

- Reduced fabric waste from minimal spaces between patterns when cutting.

- Saved costs from less fabric waste.

There are many other pattern-related technologies out there that can achieve similar benefits that brands can tap into for both digital and physical garments. These benefits can be extended to the changing of business models too as all of the elements in this case would be digitized, allowing a more streamlined experience that can easily connect to each step of the prototyping and manufacturing phases. This will also be determined by the existing systems of the brands as the integration of these technologies needs to be compatible or at least actually beneficial to them. Each brand would need to assess their own systems to determine the most efficient and effective technology to implement.

3.4. On-Demand Prototyping and Manufacturing

Not only to save fabric waste but also to save money for the brand. By having the digital patterns discussed in the previous section, digital tech packs can be made much easier and quicker while allowing clearer communication between the brand and their manufacturers. Other areas are also indirectly positively impacted such as the smoothening of the product lifecycle management (PLM) systems. This becomes a more streamlined process for production that opens the door for a business model that tackles overproduction. We consider on-demand manufacturing here where less units can be made per style as a positive impact by the opportunities brought by AI, scanning software, etc. This means a brand only produces a product when an order has been received. The traditional process of this (where on-demand is not possible) usually involves multiple units being produced by the brand to then later store in their physical inventory while trying to sell all of them. Being connected to the right manufacturers is key in this case, as minimum order quantities are usually in the hundreds to make it worth it for the production businesses. The customer journey would look like this:

1. Order and purchase an item on the brand online store.

2. The brand begins production of the item (it usually takes longer lead time up to delivery).

3. The brand delivers the item.

Microsoft has previously explored this area of on-demand manufacturing through a startup incubated within the company. The startup focused on technology that could reinforce the abilities of on-demand orders by fashion brands to their customers while also working toward lower minimum order quantities with similar streamlining digital elements previously mentioned. We have interviewed the founder of this startup, Kitty Yeung, and went through how this type of structure was possible. She also illustrated in Figure 3-4 the balance between production quantity and the time period, indicating that the future will hopefully become easier for this on-demand business model through more digitized processes while also positively contributing to the circular economy, which will be discussed later in Section 3.6.

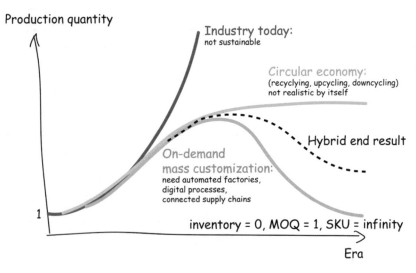

Figure 3-4. *The state of clothing manufacturing and the evolution of fashion industry by Kitty Yeung*

3.4.1. Insider Perspective: Developing an On-Demand Manufacturing Tech Solution. Interview with Kitty Yeung, Senior Director at Browzwear (Formerly Founder at Fashion Tech Incubation at Microsoft)

VR: Kitty, tell me a bit about how you got into fashion tech.

KY: When I started working in fashion, it was actually a hobby – making clothes by hand and designing. Then, I started making clothes with technologies embedded in them. I investigated the manufacturing of these wearables, and then from there, I noticed that the process is so difficult, and so much back and forth involved. I also discovered that many processes that I could do by hand were nonexistent in the workflow of the typical manufacturing factories, including embedding electronics in the clothes. My first batch went through development between nine months and over a year!

It was a little bit surprising for me because I come from the tech world; I could usually draw something and get it manufactured much easier and faster since the factories are all already set up for these sorts of processes. So I thought why can't we do the same thing for fashion? This is when the idea of using digital tools, such as 3D digital simulation, sparked for my own designs. Pretty much an end-to-end of building my own fashion brand.

Having learned everything from designing to prototyping to manufacturing at this point, I knew I could provide something that would be helpful to other independent fashion brands and potentially expand this to help the entire industry altogether. That's where I felt that Microsoft, as a big company, could help.

VR: So how did you start that journey within Microsoft?

KY: It was a really long development. It's interesting that most people do not see fashion as a technical field, especially in the engineering community. But then I realized that if I can communicate to my colleagues that fashion is actually all about technical skills needed to produce things, then people will realize that this is something that we, as engineers, can help with. So I started building an internal community through our annual hackathon. We began experimenting with our latest tooling of digital processing, computer vision, and everything put together to help bring a different type of supply chain. I started in 2018, and every year I was working on this part time with my colleagues from different backgrounds all voluntarily. Then I got funding late 2021 to work on this project full time. It's a bit like a small startup inside a big company.

VR: At the very top-line level, take us through the solution itself.

KY: It is to help the end-to-end process with the ultimate angle being on-demand mass customization. This means that the clothes are only made specifically according to their body shapes and their measurements at scale and only when there is an order. This allows very low minimum quantities for production (MOQ). Eventually, "MOQ equals one unit" is the goal that we can gradually reach. It's not going to happen right away, but that's the vision.

VR: What is your definition of fashion technology? Also, you mentioned that you had funding from Microsoft internally. Did they even understand what fashion tech was when you presented this idea to the board?

KY: It is not easy to get a tech company to understand this kind of project as corporations primarily make money by selling their existing digital tools. It took a bit of explaining for them to believe in the idea.

When defining fashion tech, for me, it means two things:

1. One is literally embedding technology in clothing, so wearable tech.

2. Two would be applying technologies in production of fashion – using digital tools and then making a digital tech pack that can be directly sent to manufacturers who also use a digital setup, configuring their machines and getting the factory as streamlined and as automated as possible.

The latter is more relatable with the work with Microsoft. So it's more like the verticals of a workforce – efficiency, productivity, tooling, and the transformation of traditional workflow.

VR: For Microsoft, is it a case where they just want to develop another product to sell or is there something else there, as to why they really believed in this specific idea?

KY: It's both. We had to convince them that we had a scalable business model, especially in the corporate world where profits are important, but also that we can make a positive impact on society and sustainability.

VR: What would you say are specifically the top challenges that don't currently allow more fashion brands to adopt on-demand manufacturing?

KY: We spoke to many design schools, designers, and manufacturers, and there is a feedback loop where designers want to come up with something new but manufacturers push back for various reasons, including minimum quantities not being matched. Also, without the help of digital fashion, designers need physical reference samples, which take time to make. All these friction points in traditional processes at every step are preventing a bigger, faster adoption of the right on-demand model.

VR: You've been working with digital design partners like Browzwear (whom you have now joined) and the Fashion Innovation Agency. How have they been key in terms of their collaboration to help you shape your solution?

KY: It was really helpful to work with them. We did not want to replace any of these 3D software; instead, we are helping connect them with the rest of the demand of the supply chain. They provide the 3D simulation capabilities for clothing; thus, the on-demand "one piece at a time" model is possible, from digital to physical.

VR: What's next then for you?

KY: I learned a tonne from my incubation and found repeatable and scalable business models to create new revenue channels for the fashion industry. I want to continue building on my past work in fashion tech so

I'm pursuing it through better suited platforms. The rapid development of AI is enabling the digital, on-demand, and customization processes that were not possible before.

It's clear that the benefits are there:

1. Either you invest in the technologies to use for production to impact the time, cost, and sustainability.

2. Or you invest in technologies that help aid on-demand orders while providing personalized items at the same time.

3. Or invest in mass production of your garments and then use the desired technology as a marketing tool or retail catalyst to sell more of them.

Any of these options will impact costs related to warehouse rentals, quantities produced, and usage/subscriptions of the technologies. One thing that they all have in common is that they allow the business models of fashion brands to become much leaner. On-demand orders mean less production; AI lay planning/related systems mean less wasted fabrics, etc.

3.5. Identifying the Garment: Transparency and Traceability

Customers have become more conscious of their purchases with many going "out of their way to buy secondhand items and to look for clothing made with environmentally friendly material" (McKinsey, 2022). This reveals that brands have more accountability to pay attention to when creating and distributing items. Reports by Statista and Mckinsey have shown the significance of the communication from the brands to their customers to clearly (and honestly) share details of the origins of the garments – from the fabrics used to the manufacturers of the fastenings. This can often be difficult as there are various suppliers who need verification in the process that brands are not always able to trace even for themselves to then pass on to their customers. For example, 'how is the fabric supplier paying attention to their ethics and sustainability goals when forming the fabrics that make up the garment purchased by the customer, etc.?'

This is the reason for introducing new legislations such as the anti-waste law for a circular economy (AGEC) in January 2023 in France to help companies become more transparent. The law will be explored deeper in Section 4.4.2, but generally, what this new law means specifically for fashion brands is that

1. Their products need to be more genuinely sustainable according to the fabrics and impact on the environment.

2. They need to be more transparent since now labeling on these products must be more accurate to reference the carbon impact according to the location of manufacturing. This is described by Paul de Montclos, president of France Terre Textile, as *"a revolution… [that] makes the textile precursor of transparency to the consumer"* (Montclos, 2022). This intends to eradicate or at least try to lessen the greenwashing that continues to be a problem in the fashion industry as discussed in Chapter 4, where brands often oversell their promises of being sustainable while their practices don't match.

This won't completely remove the problem of lack of transparency by brands; however, technology can support the value behind such legislations and activities.

Blockchain is one of the most interesting bases that allows tools to build on top of it for transparency and is a *"secure database shared across a network of participants, where up-to-date information is available to all participants at the same time"* (McKinsey, 2022). According to the McKinsey 2022 research, blockchain is broken down into the following business benefits:

– Reduced risk and lower compliance costs.

– Cost-efficient transactions.

– Automated and secure contract fulfillment.

These benefits are possible through the way that blockchain works behind the scenes when the data is collected to then later be visible when triggered by the public. When interviewing the co-founder and CEO of Qbrics, Rakesh Ramachandran described this technology as "building a trust network" (Ramachandran, 2023). Qbrics is a startup focusing on the digital workflow on blockchain to allow brands critical control and certification for their products and services. Qbrics has worked with vintage goods and collectibles where certification is crucial to prove authenticity and even the product life after purchase can be tracked. Ramachandran has broken down the process on making this possible in general to allow data to be viewed "block by block" when a brand chooses to have their products and services certified on the blockchain:

1. Convert non-digital data to digital and process it from the multiple sources it comes from (e.g., prices, remaining stock, etc.) with experts through APIs and integrators/adaptors.

2. The blockchain, which is referred to here as the golden power, with all of the various data for the one product or service, then can push out the "true data."

3. The user interface in the physical format (such as the QR code or the Spectrometer by Aware, which will shortly be explored) is made as the tactile prompt that triggers the data to be shown to the users.

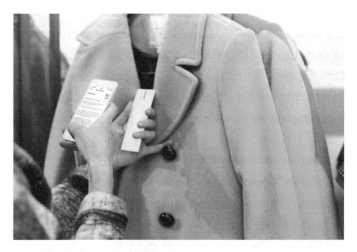

Figure 3-5. *Clear Fashion swing tag scanned on garment being scanned (QR code not visible for privacy purposes)*

Digital IDs are one of the ways to view this certified data as it usually links directly to blockchain and are triggered through QR codes hanging as swing tickets from products, such as in Figure 3-5. These are scannable to view the information stored on the digital ID concerning where the fabrics and fibers are from, who manufactured them, etc. For example, transparency tech Clear Fashion is a French app that enables brands to have their product and brand data processed so that consumers can understand their sustainability credentials. In essence, this stops vagueness and, to a certain degree, greenwashing, which will be explored further in Chapter 4. When concerning Clear Fashion specifically, they also offer a score system based on the components of the garments in 4 categories: human, health, environment & animals.

As previously mentioned, tracked information like this is difficult to obtain as a brand. For example, when brands purchase fabrics for their products, they aren't always able to know the full journey that it has gone through from the specific manufacturers to the environmental impact. This is why companies such as Aware exist. Their focus is to bring physical authentication to the blockchain with their scanners and tracers. Through this, brands are able to be verified for their use of sustainable textiles and the production journey. This authentication process starts directly with the fabric mills and spinners that the brands work with where Aware begins tracing the process from the start of the value chain including materials used, their environmental impact, countries passed through, and which manufacturers.

To keep an accurate trace of the aforementioned, a small dose of powder visible in Figure 3-6a by Aware is embedded into the raw fibers, which makes it traceable throughout the rest of the supply chain. The powder is particularly an interesting solution with its almost completely unnoticeable properties that can later be scanned and tracked all the way to when the garment has been made. This is what they refer to as *"a simple and transparent supply chain with no dirty secret"* (Warmerdam, 2023).

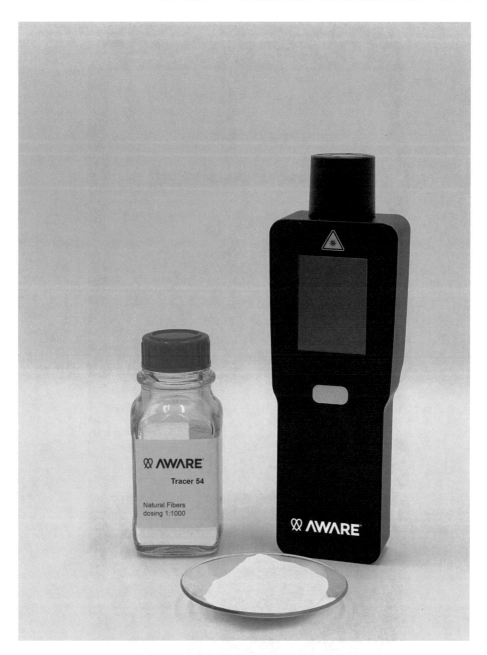

Figure 3-6a. *Powder by Aware alongside the spectrometer*

Figure 3-6b. *Screenshot of digital passport details on Aware platform*

The powered fibers are developed into fabrics and later sewn into garments that are sold in the stores. By a simple scan with the Aware scanner called the Spectrometer (on the right in Figure 3-6a), there is reassurance of the ethical and sustainable process of the above. The tick that appears on the screen (shown in Figure 3-6b) after the scanning verifies the detecting of the traceable powder that would have been embedded in the fibers earlier in the production process before the garment itself was made. All finer details of this journey (Figure 3-6c) that can be viewed on the digital passport are stored on the blockchain to remain uneditable from there.

Figure 3-6c. *Screenshot of digital passport details on Aware platform*

While brands may find this interesting to prove their traceability, this solution is only currently available for purchase directly from participating fabric suppliers. Eager brands are still able to contact their suppliers to join this service and offer this transparency. Solutions like these are beneficial to both fashion brands and suppliers for similar reasons:

1. Clients get reassured of the "behind the scenes" of the production processes.

2. Records are held on the blockchain for further validation, leaving no room for greenwashing.

3. Reputation of the brand using this tool is uplifted by this validation, and the trust is built between them and the customer.

3.6. End of Life

Circular economy strategies are coming into full effect for many fashion brands, which deciding what to do with products once their life is coming to an end is an issue that many sustainability teams are trying to figure out. Within the years of 2010 to 2020, the product end of life has been dealt with by resale platforms facilitating a peer-to-peer transaction of sale of goods that customers no longer want. Vestiaire Collective, Vinted, and Poshmark are excellent examples of platforms that have successfully scaled and managed to keep products at all market levels in circulation. Brands have also launched their own dedicated resale platforms such as Patagonia's Worn Wear. However, many products still end up in the landfill or are sent to incinerators. Even resold garments will eventually reach a definite end of life once the product has broken down from over-usage. This is where recycling as an end-of-life solution will be of importance. Technologies to support the recycling of textiles and garments are yet to be fully commercially viable at scale, as with AltMat earlier, a significant amount of financial resources and hard tech advancements is required to make it happen. However, they demonstrate signs of progress with garment recycling companies suggesting reaching expected capacities within the next ten years.

3.6.1. Disassembly and Recycling

Of the 150 billion garments that are produced each year, many of these products do not have circularity baked into the design of the item (we'll talk more about the ingredients of circularity in Chapter 4). This is where technology is making headway in ensuring that fashion can be sustainable at the product development and production level. Resortecs is one company that is aiming to make products truly circular. The company has developed hardware and industrial processes to make fashion product recycling easy by automating the disassembly of multi-material textile products that can then be fed into next stages of recycling as pure waste streams. This means that a product is completely disassembled from all of its components. Cédric Vanhoeck, founder of Resortecs, created the solution having realized that approximately 80% of a product's impact is defined at the design phase and much more waste created due to incorrect prototyping.

Vanhoeck explains to us that the Resortecs solution (Figure 3-7a) is in-built into (1) the upstream phase of fashion with his Smart Stitch (Figure 3-7b) thread that is fully dissolvable and (2) the downstream phase whereby Smart Disassembly (Figure 3-7c) industrial "ovens" are used to apply thermal and mechanical loads to discarded products. *"A product just falls apart. The smart disassembly systems ensures that all the components that were previously stitched together with Smart Stitch Sewing Thread are separated, and the benefit of the process is that it doesn't change anything in design and manufacturing because you can just swap the bobbin from the regular stitching thread bobbin"* (Vanhoeck, 2022).

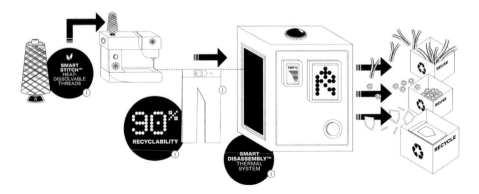

Figure 3-7a. *Resortecs solution diagram*

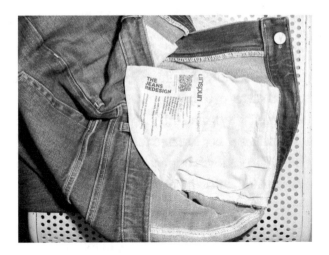

Figure 3-7b. *Resortecs x Unspun Jeans Smart Stitch label*

Figure 3-7c. *Smart Disassembly oven*

Although recycling is not new, current mechanical processes destroy garments by shredding items whole; therefore, materials are not separated, causing recycling issues. Vanhoeck believes that new innovations such as his allow brands to remain flexible and highly creative. In turn, brands can develop performance-led products while still having the ability to bake in recyclability right from the start. Resortecs partnered with French sporting goods retailer Decathlon to develop recyclable ski jackets (Figure 3-7d) that utilized their multilayered water repellent material. For the jacket to be performance driven, trims were required that cannot be recycled; thus, the Smart Thread was utilized to separate out the main textile from the trims. The jackets entered the market late 2022, and it is estimated that it will take around five years for them to return into the Decathlon system for recycling.

Fast fashion retailer Bershka, part of Inditex Group, also launched a collection of denim jeans and shorts in partnership with Resortecs (Figure 3-7e), demonstrating that recycling innovations can also be applied at high street level. Vanhoeck notes that his hardware solution can be strengthened by digital solutions such as passports whereby garments are easily identified and materials are listed. We can start to understand how the supply chain can be connected considering Aware's traceability technology and how it could be combined with Resortec's. However, the ecosystem will take time to develop: *"as the EU directive is not implemented as a local or EU legislation to have digital passports on garments, brands are not willing to invest $0.50 per garment for RFID tech to enable digital passports and place physical products into a digital system that is not yet used"* (Vanhoeck, 2022). On the flip side, Resortecs shows promise; it is five times faster and ten times cheaper than manual disassembly, multiple products can be disassembled at once, and it can be rolled out to billions of fashion products by 2028.

Figure 3-7d. *Resortecs x Decathlon ski jacket*

Figure 3-7e. *Resortecs x Bershka collection*

We know that there's a solution for disassembling products more efficiently and there are biofibers that can be recycled as mentioned at the start of the chapter; recycling is needed to give new life to the said elements. Recycling can be done in the form of mechanical and chemical depending on the product that is being handled. Refact, a garment recycling startup, utilizes both. In conversation with co-founder Pauline Guesné, she boldly states that from her findings, *"that less than 1% of any used textiles, whether it's a garment or not, is recycled into usable textile"* (Guesné, 2022), and this inspired her to create an end-to-end recycling solution. Already in the textile space with Induo, their fabric with proprietary technology for sweat and stain management, non-iron, self-cleaning, and antibacterial properties, product purpose, and end of life was at the forefront for the next innovation. However, Guesné is quite candid about how they entered the recycling space naively, which led them to spend two years on R&D and €150,000 of their own personal money to develop the first pilot. To us, this is not unusual to see such a lengthy and costly process as we often see this with the founders that we work with trying to develop bleeding edge technologies, and as echoed throughout this chapter.

The two years of research have been perfected into the following process (shown in Figure 3-7f):

> Step 1: Aggregate the used garments and textiles from third-party suppliers. The garments including trims (buttons, sequins, etc.) are tested for recyclability.
>
> Step 2: The garments are shredded up to five times.
>
> Step 3: Shredded materials are discolored and chemically changed.
>
> Step 4: Extract cellulosic material and polyester grains ready for regeneration.

The whole process currently takes two days in which everything that is cellulosic and polyester-like can be recycled to form new cotton-like fiber ready for spinning into yarns (Figure 3-7g). The resulting fibers are 100% recycled and 100% recyclable; thus, the cycle never needs to end. Guesné didn't share exactly how the magic happens (steps 3 and 4) since this is their "secret sauce," but to us, this is just the beginning of the possibilities of recycling. Refact is also faced with lengthy commercial rollout lead times, but brands will be able to capitalize on such facilities with fully operational pilots by 2025 and full capacity factories up by 2030.

Guesné highlights that although the end-of-life space presents many opportunities, a balance will need to be sought. For example, with the rise of secondhand fashion through popular marketplaces such as Vestiaire Collective, Vinted, and Poshmark, it will have a direct impact on the recycling ecosystem because only 10% of the used products that collection facilities receive contribute to 100% of their revenue. This means that there will be a squeeze on the quality of products that Refact relies on as a feed stream. This is not necessarily a bad thing since it does mean that general consumers are keeping products in the fashion system (refer back to Section 1.1) for longer because they are being resold as opposed to thrown away, but it's a challenge for other innovations like Refact to come to full fruition.

Figure 3-7f. *Refact process of turning old fabrics into new yarns (left to right)*

Figure 3-7g. *Refact finished yarns made into socks*

3.6.2. Repair and Upcycling

Before the time of cheap, fast fashion, and the throwaway culture that manifested in the second half of the 20th century, for centuries, humans repaired their clothing time after time, handing down fashion products from parent to child and so on. Obviously, this no longer happens, but there is still a space for repair services and its younger sibling, upcycling. Finds, a startup that we have worked with, primarily had the idea of helping the general consumer do something with their unused clothing. Their research found that the average person in Île-de-France (the area surrounding Paris) had approximately €425 worth of unused clothing sitting in the back of their wardrobes (Finds, 2020). This could be for a myriad of reasons, fit issues, damage, out of season, or simply the owner just fell out of love with that product. Regardless, the unused products have a potential afterlife that repair services can help remedy.

Online platforms have made it easier for such repair services to have a much wider reach rather than the individual having to go to their local repair store in person. Companies such as Clothes Doctor, Tilli, and Save Your Wardrobe have successfully implemented online experiences that mean that the customer can repair their fashion products to brand new status (or as close as possible) without having to leave their homes. Although the companies deal with all market levels and all types of products, it makes sense that most people will want to get their high-ticket items repaired. Save Your Wardrobe in particular can be integrated into a fashion brand's customer-facing experiences, which is an end-to-end solution, meaning any brand can use the technology.

These solutions make sense for the end customers, but what happens with products and textiles that have never left the factory or shop floor? The team at Finds has subsequently pivoted (the act of shifting a business strategy to accommodate new business opportunities) their solution to be surplus stock focused. As co-founder Andrea Herget notes, *"with repair and alterations, it was just a natural transformation to go into surplus stock management, which is in part a type of recycling"* (2022), meaning that they take unsold inventory from brands and direct them to reusable avenues such as upcycling projects (Figures 3-8a, 3-8b, and 3-8c) or to waste processing facilities (just like Refact). At present, there are approximately 30% unsold garments of the 100–150 billion produced each year due to overproduction, which equates to a value of approximately $500 billion per year (Fashion United, 2018).

The Finds solution taps into the data (stock level reports) of unsold inventory from fashion brands to automate the stock management process by utilizing AI to calculate and recommend what can be done with it: upcycle, donate, off-price sales, recycle. For example, for upcycling, the system knows that it will take fabric from three medium-length skirts to produce a waist-length tailored blazer. However, surplus stock management is still in its infancy and is not easy to scale across the supply chain: *"It's a kind of complex and long supply chain. As an innovator in fashion, you're most probably going to touch multiple stages along the supply chain. When we started out upcycling, we helped brands by advising them on circular design so that they could understand how to implement the model within their core business. We then moved onto managing the upcycling production and logistics phases, which is what brands now need the most help with"* (Herget, 2022).

End-of-life solutions are such an important aspect for the fashion industry moving forward. It is projected that circular models will grow from 3.5% of the global fashion market today to 23% by 2030 (Ellen MacArthur Foundation, 2022). Therefore, brands that are actively integrating such solutions across their entire supply chain now will be best prepared moving into the next decade, but it'll take foresight from company executives to make it happen. Luckily for Finds, as of 2022, France has made it illegal to destroy or dispose of unsold stock, which will be rolled out to the rest of the EU in 2024, and brands will be forced to adopt new processes.

Figure 3-8a. *Finds upcycled waistcoat and skirt*

Figure 3-8b. *Finds upcycled blazer*

Figure 3-8c. *Finds upcycled top*

3.7. Chapter Summary

Connecting, reconfiguring, and extracting untapped value from the fashion supply chain are a difficult and mammoth task, but it is possible if brands are willing to make the required financial and time investments. It's also necessary if brands wish to continue producing billions of products each year before the system collapses (think overproduction, overconsumption, and climate change). Technologies such as artificial intelligence can help to handle and reduce waste pre- and post-production cycles, next-generation materials and production processes should eventually replace all harmful practices, and factories will be able to evolve from linear to circular within the next few decades.

What we can learn from this chapter:

1. The fashion supply chain requires software and hardware to reconfigure it to become more advanced. This can be costly, and brands must be patient with the longer road maps for the technologies to become commercially scalable.

2. New business model opportunities are plentiful with advancements such as on-demand production platforms, traceability and transparency tools like digital IDs, and circular solutions like surplus stock management software.

3. As discussed in Section 1.1.2, for fashion to become circular, the supply chain needs to adopt technologies to handle product end of life like waste management and recycling. This is a combination of software and hardware coming together in specialist facilities.

Activity: Design your factory of the future.

Which will you consider to either help brands to be leaner or as a brand owner yourself, what will you consider to stay streamlined? Choose from Table 3-1 and consider why and how it could be useful to you.

Table 3-1. *Table with digital production platforms*

Technology type	Objective	Stage	Benefits
Digital pattern cutting For example, N-hega	AI-assisted lay planning, accurate digital patterns	Pre-production	Reduce fabric waste, improved communication
Next-generation material sourcing platforms For example, Material Exchange	Source sustainable and more Earth-friendly materials	Pre-production	Impact information readily available with easy access to material innovators
On-demand production platform For example, Drippy	3D simulation, no MOQ prototyping	Production	Prototype and test designs at speed and at low cost
Traceability tools For example, Aware	Make all products easily identifiable on their production journey	Production/post-production	Have granular details of product provenance for consumers and businesses
Surplus stock and waste management platforms For example, Finds	Understand what you can do with your waste or overproduced products	Post-production	Unlock monetary value as well as be more environmentally friendly
Recycling facilities For example, Resortecs	Turn old products into new products	Post-production	Create a circular system and benefit from the reuse of resources

CHAPTER 4

Marketing: Beyond Physical Realities

4.1. The New Tech Approach

"Marketing is all about brand differentiation. Why would we want to just cut and paste the same product for every single client? Because all brands invest millions of dollars in differentiation, they all want to be different." (Chippindale, 2022)

To be different: We've mentioned several times throughout this book that the fashion industry is highly saturated with brands and retailers; thus, they need to be different to stand out. Certainly fashion tech is making the marketing of fashion visually more exciting, emotionally triggering, and fantasy making, as what fashion is and always will be, especially at the higher market levels. These technologies include:

- Augmented reality (AR): Interactive experience that combines the real world and computer-generated content overlaid

© Von N. Ruzive and Peter Jeun Ho Tsang 2023
V. N. Ruzive and P. Jeun Ho Tsang, *Fashion Tech Applied*,
https://doi.org/10.1007/978-1-4842-9694-3_4

- Virtual reality (VR): Computer-generated content that can be interacted with through a device such as VR headsets as if it were physical

- Mixed reality (MR): Where the two realities merge together and physical and digital objects interact to form the experience

These technologies are creating the fashion worlds we all want to live in. Jonathan Chippindale's company, Holition, focuses on crafting digital campaigns for luxury brands to help them to be different, whether that's in the customer's home, at a real live fashion show, or in-store. Figure 4-1 shows one of Holition's projects with fashion brand Dunhill that created a holographic fashion show that moved the audience to tears: *"the lady next to me was quietly crying, at the end of the piece, because it was a very beautiful and moving piece. It was technology, music, location, lighting, smell. We brought it all together to almost create the anti-fashion show"* (Chippindale, 2022). Tears or not, the possibilities with all of these realities are placing fashion brands on another level.

Figure 4-1. *Dunhill holographic fashion show by Holition*

4.1.1. Fashion in Your Living Room

One thing's for sure, the prevalence of "work from home" culture is pushing innovations to fit the needs that come with it. Most of the solutions that we have spoken about so far, including digital fashion, NFTs, etc., are available at the tap of a smartphone in your living room. Beyond the live stream fashion week shows that make you feel like you are on the front row of the actual physical show, technological implementations have paved the way for even more immersive experiences with fashion.

How? Augmented reality is among the main technologies allowing this immersion. Snapchat has exploited this opportunity with many fashion brand collaborations. The collaboration with Gucci sneakers that launched in 2020 allowed users to try on their options via the Snapchat app lenses. What initially started off as a trial to simply "raise awareness for the collection" launch and "increase engagement translated into sales" (Snap Inc., 2020). Customers can see what the shoes will look like on their feet with the help of AR technology allowing tracking for the movement of the feet to still represent a "close to real life" view of the shoes on the feet from different angles in real time as shown in Figure 4-2.

Figure 4-2. *Screenshots of the Snapchat app using GUCCI virtual try-on lenses*

Simply viewing videos and photos of products on the brand's website does not seem to cut it anymore, as the Ipsos and Snapchat research shows, customers who use the AR virtual try-on feature are more likely to make purchases thereafter (Snap x Ipsos, 2023). The more interesting part of this research reveals that the keenness to use this tech is more prominent in the customers vs. the brands. The role of the customer is to simply use the tech, while the brands need to do the background work of developing or collaborating with the appropriate company to make the tech possible, which could be the reason for the differing demands between the two parties. Irrespective of the potential reasons for this mismatch, the fact remains that not all brands are investing in this technology (dare we say, "yet").

One thing with virtual try-ons that remains lacking is the link with the body measurements of the user for a more end-to-end use case and user experience. So far, most virtual try-ons remain strictly visual, making it more of a visual representation of the physical product and a suggestion of what it may look like when wearing it as opposed to being an accurate representation of the fit of the real garment or product. While this may be the case, influencers benefit from this predominantly visual use of tech as the focus is more about marketing a digital garment which they usually would need to purchase multiple physical garments that may cost more in comparison according to the brands they buy from.

For virtual try-on to move further from a merely visual representation of the final products, it must marry with the technologies that would also allow the digital garments to represent how the items would fit on the user. Most startups are currently focusing on one or the other solution; however, putting them together could become revolutionary. The result of this would be necessary to put more weight on the use cases of brands adopting the virtual try-on. For example, customers gaining visual results for what the garments would potentially look like *as well as* the measurements of how the garments would fit in real life along with recommendations of the sizes to order, would shift to a more thorough virtual try-on between the needs of the customer regarding fit and potentially more sales for the brands. It would go beyond just a visual representation.

4.1.2. Alternative Online Immersive Experience with AR and AI

Augmented reality (AR) is enabling more than just virtual try-on. It has been expanded to other interactions between the customers and the fashion brands. There is a full scope of what can be offered when using AR for customer retention and marketing. This includes the use of AR holograms that allow another view of fashion products within a customer's own space. The SaaS solution, Cappasity, has focused on this as they drive fast production 3D and AR content. This is one that has changed the way we can view items on the smartphone giving a hyperreal overview of the products similar to what we observed in the digital fashion items section, but this time, the process is quite different and, arguably, more human focused. Typically, these are AR holograms created in the following steps:

1. Record a short 4K quality video of the product rotating on a spinning platform to capture the 360-degree view of an item.

2. The footage is then edited to remove the background to keep the product as the sole item on the screen later on.

3. The video is converted into frames per millisecond to allow the movement of the item at each frame later on.

4. This is then converted into an AR hologram.

The result is ultimately an interactive capture that plays on a loop (according to the rotation the item was recorded as), with the ability to be moved with a finger on the phone screen at any of these different frames as an AR hologram. The process is fairly simple compared to the creation of the digital twins previously explored, as it relies on the capturing of a physical final product that has already been produced instead of creating one digitally from scratch. There is more emphasis on the video editing here as opposed to a digital twin that would typically rely on the pattern, digital fabrics, digital rendering, and other potential finishing elements including the avatar. "What could usually take weeks to create with an alternative process, is created within as little as 20 minutes per SKU with this solution" (Minina, 2023).

When moving on to the practical use between the holograms and the virtual try-on, it is that it mainly showcases the product as a 3D AR hologram that is representative of the real-life item. It does not have the same interactivity as the virtual try-on. Instead of seeing what the tried-on garment or product may potentially look like on the customer through the screen, this time the focus is on the interactivity with the AR hologram product to view it in a place that is familiar to them as an alternative marketing campaign. The interactivity begins from having the smartphone activating its back-facing camera to display on the screen what is being captured, which becomes the backdrop of the AR hologram product. The process outlined before would then become important for this part to remain as clean as possible, including the proper removal of the background as well as a video that would have been captured as a smooth loop to discourage any glitches.

Von having collaborated with Cappasity for her own inclusive fashion brand, she experienced this firsthand from the development stage to embedding this on her online store. The main purpose of this collaboration was for the customers to experience her clothing designs in AR in a different way to the norm. This campaign was in the form of a competition for the public to get involved by posting their own screenshots of their experience with the AR holograms of the collection. The intention was to allow more potential customers to be attracted to joining the competition as they see their peers posting their screenshots on social media (the main entry requirement). This would eventually create a ripple effect where the garments being showcased would also catch the attention of the potential customers as the AR hologram allowed them to view the main feature of the garments, in particular the blazer that had an unconventional way of opening – something that a still image wouldn't have as much of an impact in comparison.

Figure 4-3a. *Von Ruz brand in the process of capturing a rotating model*

Figure 4-3b. *Camera capturing a model in Von Ruz clothing in a 4K video*

Figure 4-3c. *Von Ruz brand showcasing AR hologram via Cappasity*

The general reaction of the users was the foreseen "oh that's cool," with more traffic being driven to the social media platform of the brand compared to the traffic driven to the website in this scenario. Either way, what this revealed was the importance of dwell time during marketing efforts such as these. Elina Minina, CBDO and co-founder at Cappasity, mentioned that these kinds of marketing efforts are *"not always about making as many sales as possible, but there is also importance in simply encouraging more time for a customer to look at the products"* (2023) through these technologies. Dwell time means more time spent looking at the product details and at least more awareness created for the concerned product as "it's crucial for the brand to allow online shoppers to study every detail of their unique products" (Minina, 2023). Claris Virot, one of Cappasity's brand clients, noticed a significant increase in customer engagement: on average, their visitors now spend an extra 19 seconds browsing products and 26 seconds viewing the most popular bags. This can still indirectly result in a purchase later on which other collaborating established brands have experienced too:

> *"Among Cappasity clients are such brands as Marine Serre, Polène, Jazmin Chebar, Claris Virot, and many more. Their experience has shown that immersive content makes online shopping interactive, improves customer experience, reduces returns, and in some cases increases sales by more than 30%." (Minina, 2023)*

What if we took this visual AR technology into AI? This is the case for 3DLOOK that has combined a few features in one with the aim to get closer to what we previously saw as fragmented solutions in Section 4.1, where one solution focuses on trying on garments while the other focuses on providing measurements. Both elements are important, which is why it is interesting to see solutions that aim to target the mix. Using AI as the back-end technology for this solution is what allows the two to merge in this case. This has meant that the visual element is static instead of live in this scenario after capturing the customer first for the virtual try-on part of the solution. From this to the size recommendations, 3DLOOK has successfully touched on different elements that impact the online "at-home" shopping experience in two ways:

1. Static virtual try-on embedded on a brand's website where you can see yourself from two photos that you would have taken (instead of a live try-on we saw earlier in Section 4.1.1).

2. AI measuring tool that gathers eight measurements
    that then match to the sizing chart of the brand
    to provide a size recommendation as shown in
    Figure 4-4.

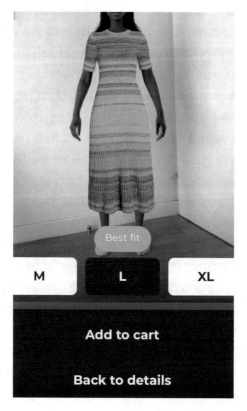

Figure 4-4. *Von trying out the 3DLOOK AI mobile body scan*

Solutions like these can also self-improve their intelligence with the more data collected over time. The data collected can train the algorithm according to the measurements obtained per brand for better sizing recommendations. This data goes back to the brand to keep them informed of their customer base. While this does not completely respond to the gap between live virtual try-on and size recommendations combined (due to the try-on being static based from two photos), it is one of the closest solutions for this need. When speaking with the CEO of 3DLOOK, Vadim Rogovskiy, it was clear that this technology was particularly useful when the closures of fitting rooms in 2020 were in their prime, with approximately 60,000 customers having scanned during that year during their trial with the sales reps. The data collected from the measurements not only benefited the customers for the recommendations but also the *"back-end which would let the brands know more about their customer's morphologies"* and further helps reduce returns through offering the most common fit, as *"the only way to really solve the problem of returns is to understand how your customer looks, their average measurements and buying habits"* (Rogovskiy, 2023). Like us, Rogovskiy believes that within the next ten years plus, this type of technology will help to further personalize e-commerce where the usual journey is followed through from *"the try-on to the ads on social media revolving around your image with the products instead of the models this time, helping to continue marketing to the customer after the try-on itself"* (Rogovskiy, 2023).

This tells us one thing, that fashion tech solutions still have an opportunity to eventually become an all-rounder solution to implement into brands, as opposed to being fragmented as they currently are. We can see that this also depends on which back-end technology that the tech startup or company specializes in and the capabilities of it. This is perhaps a "jack of all trades, master of none" scenario where tech startups and companies are currently staying focused on their own expertise before trying to perfect multiple solutions in one tool. This opens the door for collaborations within these companies to provide an end-to-end solution for the differing needs (in this case, visual as well as measurements) for brands to adopt as one package.

When regarding the marketing efforts, AR and AI solutions discussed are interesting to experience "in the living room" as it brings the usual fitting room or products into your own space with little effort required to get the upclose visual details or measurements. While this is great for customers, adopting new technologies for marketing purposes can still have a pushback by the brands that need to adopt them first. Minina describes this as *"brands [being] overwhelmed with basic tasks and adjustments [for their usual business activities]. So they often lack the resources to implement such important features as ours. Besides, with multiple departments involved in the negotiation process, it usually takes enterprises considerable time to implement new technology"* (2023). When considering the smaller brands, the AR holograms can be costly too as all of the steps listed plus the hosting require funds. This is why Cappasity continues to build their suite of solutions including their 3D views that are also rotatable and allow the interactivity without the additional steps required to appear on a website as Figures 4-5 and 4-6 shown, as opposed to the AR. This is also a simpler capturing process that can be done with the resources that a brand already has; for example, instead of a rotatable platform for capturing, the videographer can rotate around the product or model. The purpose of the outcome becomes slightly different in this case as it focuses on altering the typical static e-commerce imagery as opposed to offering the immersive experience seen in Figure 4-3c.

Figure 4-5. *Von Ruz clothing shown as 3D views by Cappasity. Rotatable on the website* `www.vonruz.com`

Figure 4-6. *Marine Serre garments in 3D view rotatables by Cappasity on website*

The brands that do pick up solutions like these bring the products to their customer as opposed to the other way round. We will see further in the next section where the customer is required to leave the house to experience the other marketing tools by other technologies.

4.2. In-Store Marketing

We can see that there are physical vs. digital experiences vs. the fusion of both when categorizing the fashion marketing efforts that are enhanced with tech. This next section may help to further pull this apart when concerning the use cases in stores, specifically for marketing purposes. Let's break it down into technologies used in these ways:

Table 4-1. *Digital vs. physical vs. merge chart*

Digital spaces	Physical spaces	Used in both digital *and* physical
AI/VR/AR for immersive marketing efforts on smartphones/websites/metaverse. Previously explained as accessible in the comfort of your home in the previous section	AI/VR/AR used in physical stores or pop-ups, which will be explored further in Chapter 5. Ultimately the same technologies that are accessible at home but serving as an attention grabber in physical spaces	Technologies that can be applied to either scenario for a combined experience

In this case, we must look into why stores would adopt the third option, specifically during marketing efforts. The tech becomes the centerpiece of the marketing campaign, where the focus is on showcasing the technology itself without necessarily expecting the customers to make any purchases. In other words, it's about displaying the concerned products in eye-catching ways to increase more awareness of the technologies with a similar aim to increase dwell time as per Section 4.1.2.

Von experienced this type of marketing campaign activation at Galeries Lafayette on the Champs-Elysées, Paris (Figure 4-7b), when the Web3 company, Lablaco, installed their metaverse space in the center of the physical department store (Figure 4-7a). The department store is one of the most visited globally among others such as Selfridges from the UK and Macy's from the United States, selling all fashion categories from lifestyle products to footwear and everything in between. The collaboration with Galeries Lafayette, among many other partnerships they have previously orchestrated, meant that the fashion designers who are part of their

12-month accelerator would be showcased during the installation. Through this program, such marketing efforts and other support become the backbone for the emerging brands entering into the metaverse.

While some passers-by were staring at the technology and pop-up, others decided to get right into the experience. The full experience consisted of the following:

In the metaverse at the store:

- Collaboration between Lablaco and fashion designers by showcasing the digital garments in their curated metaverse space called Spin.Fashion.

- The fashion designs were available to be purchased as phygitals: they were available as a physical garment and/or as an NFT alone (same design but digital only).

- Customers could try on the digital garments with their selected avatar inside the Oculus Quest with the help of other features, such as digital mirrors in the metaverse to mirror the real-life experience of seeing yourself in a physical mirror.

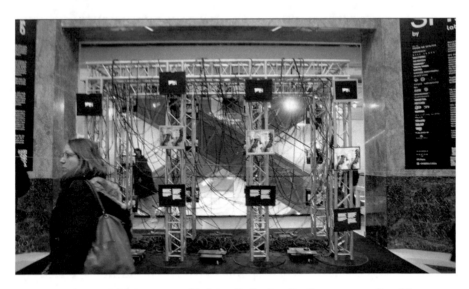

Figure 4-7a. *Lablaco installed in Galeries Lafayette on the Champs-Elysées, Paris*

Figure 4-7b. *Von using Spin.Fashion in VR at Galeries Lafayette on the Champs-Elysées, Paris*

Physically at the store (while still tapping into the digital):

- QR codes on screens that would lead to their standard digital platform on their website Web2 platform and access the AR version of the store/installation itself on smartphones. This would show as a filter on the phone to see what is being exposed in their metaverse space.

- Multiple Oculus Quest stations for the customers to visit and try the Spin.Fashion metaverse space by Lablaco as this was their main project.

None of the designers being showcased were physically selling at Galeries Lafayette like the usual brands that sell there; therefore, this meant that the focus was more on the installation itself and these external brands. When speaking with the co-CEO and founder of Spin.Fashion, it became clear that the purpose of such collaborations was to test the solution. The ability to simply plug and play this type of installation at any space means that the testing doesn't require too much commitment from the store. Meanwhile, the small collaborating brands being showcased in the VR have access to a prestigious marketing opportunity on a street that attracts 300,000 international and local visitors per day (Galeries Lafayette ChampsElysées, 2019).

4.2.1. Insider Perspective: Immersive virtual reality experiences at physical stores. Interview with Lorenzo Albrighi, co-CEO and founder at Spin.Fashion

VR: What was the interest of this collaboration for all parties involved?

LA: For Galeries Lafayette specifically, they had been looking around for tech solutions for a while. They were excited about the fact that Spin. Fashion is an end-to-end solution that provides the opportunity to plug into easily, meaning the ability to test our product without needing to figure it all out from their side. Our emerging brands from the program were able to gain exposure from being showcased at a prestigious store that they normally wouldn't be able to access.

VR: What are the key indicators that came from this collaboration?

LA: We featured 37 designers from all over the world and

- Sold just under 1000 NFTs during the installation

- 99% of these customers had never previously owned an NFT

- 230,000 participants tried out the overall experience in store

- And 3.9 million virtual try-ons (from the Web2 and Web3 spaces)

VR: To which extent is the commitment to fashion tech by industry leaders in the established fashion corporations you partner with?

LA: We have different levels of partnerships with our platforms, which include sponsorships by the corporations. All the partners are selected carefully according to their genuine dedication to circularity. All of their support is directly concerning monetary contributions toward our 12-month program and extending to all of our support activities such as the pop-up.

VR: What should we expect from the future of Lablaco and Spin. Fashion?

LA: We have recently agreed to showcasing at VivaTech 2023, which is a place that does not normally dedicate much of its space to fashion technologies, so it's great to finally have this kind of platform where we can share our expertise with the large number of visitors. We also continue growing our partnerships for the future Circular Fashion System Summit in the metaverse.

4.3. There's No Longer the Need for Physical Samples to Sell

Fashion has developed a formula for the buying and selling seasons. This happened ever since the first days of the catwalk show in the early 1900s and designers using samples to sell to the client as opposed to the designer crafting bespoke items with the client on-site. The physical sample, regardless of whether it's displayed on the catwalk, in a presentation, or at a showroom, has been a key tool for marketing campaigns. Some industry professionals may even argue that there's no fashion week without the physical samples ready for showcasing. But is this true nowadays?

As discussed in Chapter 3, a single style may go through at least two to four sample iterations prior to the marketing-ready version for presentation. When Peter was working with his clients who were small to medium-sized fashion brands in Asia, they would request between five and ten "salesman samples," or in other words, the sample ready to show to buyers or shot in marketing campaigns. These were shipped to various locations, showrooms, and wholesale agents around the world. Imagining a medium-sized collection of around 100 styles, then that's a lot of samples adding up. However, the COVID-19 pandemic has begun to dismantle the notion that physical samples are needed for effective marketing and selling to happen. Digital samples and showrooms have now become so realistic, experiential, tactile, and quite frankly sophisticated enough to be just as effective. One person that believes this is Anne-Christine Polet who leads Stitch.

4.3.1. Digital and Virtual B2B Showrooming

Physical showrooms have been a popular way for buyers to find products that match the brands or department stores that they are representing. The decision-making and purchasing experience usually looks like this:

1. Schedule an appointment with the brand's sales team, or a third-party sales agent.

2. Attend a physical appointment at the brand's showroom.

3. Browse items (often with the brand representative).

4. Try them on or see worn on a fit model.

5. Select items to purchase.

6. Place a purchase order (PO) outlining the SKUs (short for stock keeping units, which denote a unique reference code to that product style) and quantities, etc.

Buyers often fly across countries for this one-to-one physical experience at showrooms to get a closer look at the items they are purchasing before committing to them, which can also be after seeing them on models at a fashion show. This puts more weight on the expectation for brands to deliver satisfying experiences during these appointments and opens up the opportunity to reconsider the standard process. While it may seem relevant to implement technologies such as AR virtual try-ons on screens in the physical showrooms, this experience has in fact completely been digitized, which would no longer require the need for buyers to be physically present at the showrooms. This has opened up the digital and virtual showrooms.

Stitch is an intrapreneurial startup (like we saw earlier with Kitty and Microsoft) born out of the brand Tommy Hilfiger, in which Anne-Christine Polet took the challenge of digitizing the internal buying and selling processes. She describes Stitch as a fashion tech company that helps brands digitize their value chain by helping them create, develop, and showcase their collections in 3D. Aside from the physical samples, many fashion brands still use analogue practices within the wholesale process such as printed line sheets (a document outlining details of each product in a collection) created on Excel and printed lookbooks (catalogs given to buyers). The idea is that Stitch can reconfigure the foundations of the existing analogue processes.

Anne-Christine, having previously worked in Google prior to Tommy Hilfiger, understood that fashion was "old school" in comparison. However, by observing what made the sales team successful within the brand, innovation opportunities arose as to what could be digitized. This ultimately led to the decision of all the showroom floors within the Tommy Hilfiger head office in Amsterdam going fully digital. As with most new technologies, this threatened existing office dynamics. Polet recounts that there was *"reluctance from the sales team at first because they like physical samples and they think that they have the winning formula. However, suddenly, we saw brand alignments increasing. We saw merchandising alignment, so the buy alignment started increasing across the region, and then most importantly was that their selling window required was cut from 12 weeks to 6 weeks. Multiply this across 4 selling seasons each year. This was all because digital gave them so much more efficiency versus the analogue way of working with samples and remerchandising"* (Polet, 2022).

In the case of Stitch, it took several iterations of the digital showroom and selling process to perfect. Anne-Christine and her team went through around 50 iterations of the physical showroom experience including the furniture, screens, and walls. *"In the beginning we had built a showroom that had closed walls, doors and curtains, so you would go into the room, and it would only be screens (Figure 4-8a). People were becoming so claustrophobic it was insane, but also the buyers became quite anxious because they were only in a digital space. We realized that we had another showroom on that floor that had glass walls. That showroom got booked all the time whereas the other one was left empty. We realized that the glass walls made such a difference to the digital experience (Figure 4-8b)."*

Figure 4-8a. *Closed wall Stitch digital showroom*

Figure 4-8b. *Glass-walled Stitch digital showroom*

Figure 4-8c. *Stitch digital interface in an open plan showroom*

Figure 4-8d. *Stitch luxury showroom*

Stitch is a good example of how the selling of garments without the physical samples is drastically changing corporate processes. Stitch's internal success can also be attributed to the former Tommy Hilfiger CEO, who took the bold decision to roll out company-wide digitization across several floors (Figures 4-8c and 4-8d). These bold moves are quite often required by top executives to see the impact of fashion tech innovation. Results shown were as follows:

- 85% reduction of physical samples.

- Stronger brand stories and unified storytelling across teams globally.

- Increased sell-through due to shortened calendars and better response to consumer trends.

- Improved cost-efficiencies, streamlined workflows, and margins.

In the case of Tommy Hilfiger where there is the luxury of head office space, it makes sense to have a face-to-face experience. For smaller brands that may not have a physical showroom, there are other ways of presenting digitally. For example, JOOR and NuORDER are two companies delivering a fully online experience via their web-based showrooms, replacing the traditional physical lookbook, line sheet, and purchase book setup. For more experimental brands, an immersive virtual or mixed reality 3D environment may be better for brand alignment, which will be discussed later in the book. Although digital showrooming is coming to the forefront, Polet does stress that the P&L (profit and loss) owner needs to see the opportunity: *"Uptake is not as strong because the current formula still sells"* (Polet, 2022). Therefore, it will need buy-in from executives for it to become disruptive industry-wide.

The same notion was shared when Von spoke with Romain Blanco who was the General Manager at the digital showroom, Le New Black. Polet mentioned, the current physical showroom format is still favorable even by the smaller emerging fashion brands. There is a clear pushback by the hosted brands on the Le New Black platform who had been offered free support of different implementing technologies to their showrooms including digital twins, etc., that would help to showcase their collections differently. Most of the brands didn't see the value in these types of adoptions as their focus remained aspirational toward the traditional showroom experience to sell directly to buyers without any fashion tech tools in between. As of the time of writing this book, the brands prefer meeting the buyers in person and pushing their sales manually in the usual physical setting described at the beginning of this section. The most "digital" or "tech" implementations that have been accepted by these brands are the more lo-fi tech where they join the digital-only showroom that resembles an online marketplace (Blanco, 2023).

What does this say about the fashion technology choices regarding B2B marketing? While some brands are embracing technologies in other areas of the supply chain including certain elements for the marketing phase, others prefer to keep some aspects traditional. This can make it difficult for fully digital experiences to become more practiced or widely accepted across the industry for marketing activities.

4.3.2. Insider Perspective: Building Immersive Brand Experiences and Virtual Worlds. Interview with Matthew Drinkwater, Head of the Fashion Innovation Agency

Rewind to the early 2000s and games such as Second Life and The Sims introduced the globe to virtual worlds. The fashion industry was nowhere to be seen. Twenty years later brands of all sizes are realizing the potential of the virtual environment for marketing and retail purposes, extending the brand experience and bridging the gap between customer and product regardless of where they are located. Peter interviewed Matthew

Drinkwater, Head of the Fashion Innovation Agency based in London, to discuss how a brand may approach building out a virtual world and digital assets.

PJHT: How did you get into building fashion innovations and what is the Fashion Innovation Agency (FIA)?

MD: I spent a long time working for luxury brands in Japan in innovation roles, looking at how we could improve consumer experiences in-store and online in the formative days of the Internet and e-commerce. The FIA was set up to explore emerging technologies and their impact on the fashion and retail industries. We do this by looking at three main areas:

1. Design: How we can use technology to change the way designers make their collections.

2. Showcasing: How fashion can use immersive technologies: AR, VR, and mixed reality.

3. Retail: The way technology can change the way designers retail their collections and the impact on business models.

Typically, what we are doing with a lot of the technology is looking at being three to five years away from commercialization so we can begin building a narrative around what is to come.

PJHT: How did you decide on the technology focus?

MD: The first couple of years in 2013 was focused on fashion wearables when there was a buzz around integrating electronics into clothing and the Internet of Things. However, during this process, we noticed that it was not a sustainable way of creating clothing considering the technological fast pace of change. As soon as you embed a circuit into a garment, it's out of date. The smart clothing and smart textile industry moved much closer to health and well-being where you could begin to demonstrate a kind of quantifiable benefit. In those industries, pure fashion was less obvious.

In 2015, we started looking at 3D design, and we started to work with Microsoft HoloLens and Magic Leap in their very early days. From that point onward, we had this realization that immersive technologies would play an enormous part in those three main areas that we'd identified around creation, showcasing, and retailing.

PJHT: Do you think that the fashion metaverse will end up like wearables?

MD: The metaverse has started to bring back a lot of those conversations around that wearables started; sense, feeling, emotion. The sensory elements of how you feel within a virtual space and how you might improve brand experiences within that.

PJHT: Have the project partners that you've worked with been instrumental in guiding the agency's growth?

MD: They have, but probably more from a technological side than a fashion side because I don't believe that any of this will be fashion led. Fashion needs to be integral to those conversations, but technology will dictate where we go and what is possible.

PJHT: Can you share details of successful projects?

MD: We did some digitization for Mulberry that was beginning to look at what is the impact of having a fully digital product on e-commerce sites. We showed that the click-through rate was depending on product visualization. It was 20–40% higher when you had a 3D image displayed compared to a flat 2D image.

Other projects included Microsoft HoloLens in collaboration with Martine Jarlgaard (Figure 4-9a). We looked at how you can generate an emotional reaction through technology and the sense of meaning for the consumer. For us, it can have a lot of tangible benefits in terms of measurable ROI and how you can improve processes.

PJHT: Do you help fashion retailers with business strategy too?

MD: We talk about risk when we're dealing with emerging technologies. Immersive tech is still at those formative stages where things may not look as perfect as they could do, particularly through mixed reality and virtual reality. There are hardware limitations which brands need to understand and how that will affect the experiences that they want to deliver. It's effectively beginning to talk to brands about the options available. What are the pipelines required? Where do the assets sit? What skill sets do they have internally to deliver the project and what might they need in the future?

PJHT: What are the success metrics that you are accountable for?

MD: I get a little frustrated by the obsession with financial return on investment, particularly when it comes to something new; there's always an element of risk. I think back to a project that we did with a young startup that was born out of London College of Fashion called AnamXR. They delivered an immersive digital world with Pangaia where the dwell time within that experience was approximately seven minutes. When you talk about a world where you have a millisecond to capture people's attention, then every second is a tangible return on investment.

PJHT: Do you think digital fashion will ever be commercially viable to make money?

MD: I genuinely believe and have said for a long time that it will form an important revenue stream for every fashion retailer. Whether it's selling a digital form of a physical product purchased in-store or a purely digital product itself. Both of those will be important parts of any fashion retailer's business model in the future.

It's undeniable that the world is changing and the technologies that will deliver more 3D experiences (like in Figure 4-9b) in our everyday lives will become more commonplace. The real turning point will be the industry deploying intelligent decisions based on real-time data that are going to impact every kind of function within the industry. Whether you're working in buying, merchandising, or store operations, real-time data can change the entire customer journey.

Figure 4-9a. *Martine Jarlgaard attendee wearing a headset to experience the mixed reality campaign*

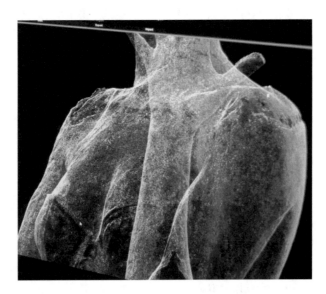

Figure 4-9b. *Sabina x Reactiv Reality campaign mixed reality holograms*

4.3.3. Multiverse Marketing

When we think of the word "multiverse," we may conjure up images associated with certain comic and sci-fi series filled with superheroes and intergalactic villains. Although there are heroes and villains in fashion, we don't mean that in this context. The metaverse is rapidly uncovering new ways of delivering content, experiences, and relationship building between the brand and consumer. The work explored by Anne-Christine and Matthew Drinkwater earlier in this section is building the foundations of the metaverse, but brands and designers do not need to stick to one style of metaverse. As the medium becomes more complex and use cases become diversified, brands may choose to deploy multiple metaverse strategies, and hence, multiverse marketing comes into play. Therefore, we can explain it as the creation of an ecosystem of multiple virtual worlds, interlinked or not, delivering digital experiences within a marketing campaign.

As Matthew Drinkwater mentions in his interview, with AnamXR, positive engagement rates are possible if the content delivered is thoughtfully considered. We delved deeper with AnamXR's CEO, Irene-Marie Seelig, to understand where the multiverse may be taking the fashion industry and what exactly is needed for brands to see a positive return. Seelig describes her platform as a *"virtual immersive multiverse that helps brands to get into the metaverse by creating their own worlds to tell stories and shop digital or physical products"* (2022). AnamXR was created as a response to her experience working in various luxury brands and observing the difficulties that they had executing digital experience: *"I thought there must be an easier way for brands to get involved in the Metaverse or in digital experiences. Back in 2018-2019, they were testing with the gaming industry, but in a rudimentary manner and I thought there has to be a better way in which brands can express themselves in a more photorealistic dimension"* (Seelig, 2022).

The need for metaverse marketing is still in its exploratory phase within fashion, but some of the advantages of using a platform such as AnamXR include the following:

1. Digital storytelling: If the brand and narratives are perfected, then the metaverse allows the viewer to fully immerse in that brand's story. This could be about a specific product, brand history, or any narrative that works better in such an environment. The potential consequences are higher engagement and retention. AnamXR's campaign with Pangaia was so successful because of the strong sense of "why" that was delivered, whereby the brand used the platform for B2C and B2B purposes, ultimately leading to strong product discovery campaigns.

2. Metaverse stores: Meta (Facebook's parent company) is spending billions on its metaverse division, Reality Labs, with approximately 20% of its spending in 2023 (Meta, 2022). This is in anticipation of the metaverse's potential. With Facebook partnering with companies such as DressX to sell digital clothing, shopping in the metaverse is expected to become the norm within the next couple of decades. For fashion brands, creating virtual stores to sell digital and physical products will be essential in capturing metaverse users. Gartner predicts that 25% of people will be spending at least one hour per day in the metaverse by 2026 (Gartner, 2022), which is a vital time to capture potential shoppers.

3. Experiences: Token gating, or in other words, restricted areas into the brand's world, is only accessible to customers that have a specific pass, which in most cases at present is an NFT of some sort. The token,

or pass, allows the holder to gain access to exclusive digital or physical products, experiences, rewards, and more. This enables hyper-targeted campaigns and ensures customers are retained. *"This is definitely a way of the future I feel as more and more brands are launching NFTs. This is how you can demonstrate and provide utility from a digital standpoint"* (Seelig, 2022).

4. IP ownership and control: The metaverse is ripe for creators as the infrastructure allows creative ideas to come to life and be deployed rapidly. Quite often the creators are also rule breakers, and as seen in the infamous legal battle over a creator's use of the Hermés Birkin bag to create MetaBirkins in early 2023, the legalities in the digital space are not quite defined. For marketeers, this is where it's better to be early and take full ownership as to how a brand is to be represented in the metaverse and to which audiences.

Multiverse marketing is not necessarily just about brands taking full control of their digital presence, but also being collaborative with the creator economy. Seelig explains that NFTs and blockchain enable brands and creators to share their IP that can be built on top of by another third-party creator. For example, music is an industry where ghost artists are used frequently and NFTs allow these professionals to also be paid royalties in a transparent manner. This can also be applied to fashion where ghost designers and creators are quite often led in the shadows.

Ultimately multiverse marketing is about selling products. However, there is not yet a set formula as to what is the most effective way to deliver a campaign in this space. At AnamXR, the company works in 45-day sprints to ensure that campaigns are delivered with up-to-date advancements since the space is rapidly changing. One such sprint was with sportswear giant Adidas and AnamXR laying the foundations for their metaverse campaign.

The proof-of-concept project entailed focusing on bringing the outdoors into the online space to drive offline sporting activities (a little paradoxical we think). This meant linking 100 products inside the metaverse to the brand's e-commerce site and building out other Web3 components such as POAP (proof-of-attendance protocol) to ensure sales as well as retention. A small-scale project for such a large brand, but these types of small campaigns are a good way for any metaverse newbie to start understanding how it could plug into their overall business strategies with elements such as IP, digital asset revenue generation, cryptocurrency, and the utility aspects.

For designers or brands looking to enter the metaverse space, partnering with an automated metaverse creation platform could be a good move for efficiency, cost, and speed factors. Seelig mentions that many of her clients come to her thinking that it's easy to enter the metaverse, but this is not the case. Aside from the 3D asset creation aspect, it's also vital to understand how to export and import files between the various platforms, how to maintain rendering quality and not lose polycounts, and ripping in scenes to create the virtual environments. In the case of Pangaia's campaign (Figures 4-10a and 4-10b), Seelig's team experimented with the navigation and gaming components to understand how to increase dwell time. Two navigation systems were deployed to capture different types of audiences, especially non-native metaverse viewers: *"we wanted to have a guided walk-through world so people could understand the products but through incentives or recognition. Like 'yes, you're doing the right thing.' At the end, if you got all the various product colors and learned all the information about them then there was a surprise."* For the brand, the objective was to increase engagement time, thus making the investment worthwhile. The same gamification framework was applied to another project that AnamXR executed with an NFT artist and a scavenger hunt style world. The result was viewers roaming for up to two hours to find all the pieces of art. In a world where attention spans are short, this demonstrates the potential power of well-thought-out metaverse worlds.

Figure 4-10a. *AnamXR and Pangaia campaign*

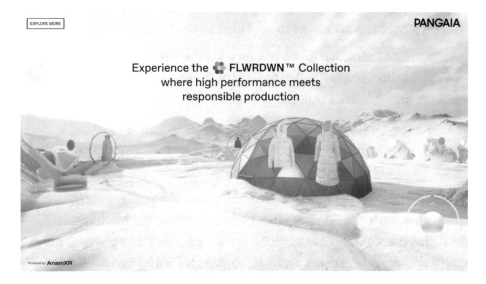

Figure 4-10b. *AnamXR and Pangaia navigation*

Going back to Holition and Tommy Factory that we started to discuss in Chapter 2, real world and metaverse were brought together for their autumn/winter 2022/2023 show. Instigated by the Chief Brand Officer and the Tommy Hilfiger Web3 team (known as 3DX), the teams knew that they wanted to integrate the element of digital fashion and multiverse marketing to make a lot of noise. This is where the Holition team came in to craft the campaign. The campaign consisted of having the physical fashion show (Figure 4-11a) run simultaneously with a virtual fashion show in the gaming platform, Roblox (Figures 4-11b and 4-11c), of exactly the same collection. To support the show itself was a whole experience created including an NFT as a POAP (as discussed earlier) and an AR experience (Figure 4-11d) around the physical runway setup. Challenges that the Holition team had to overcome to pull off the campaign were as follows:

- Timing: 45 IRL models timed in sync with the Roblox show compacted into a 12-minute show.

- Digitizing the entire collection: Approximately 700 fashion pieces that had to be digitized within a tight timeframe and budget. Tommy Hilfiger actually tapped into the Roblox community to help digitize the large collection.

- Time sensitive AR activations: Via the smartphone, balloons appeared at the end of the show with personalized name initials of the audience.

- Keeping the digital and Roblox community happy: Keeping them happy with the same level of importance as the IRL guests.

Chippindale explains that the campaign itself was a success in terms of bringing the two worlds together and storytelling, but he stresses that the digital community "*are kind of a friend and a foe.*" The physical show ran 12 minutes late due to seating celebrities, meaning that the Roblox show also ran late: "*Tommy Hilfiger learned that you've got to respect the online community as much as you do the VIP's in real life. If you're going to invite people into your world, you've got to treat them properly. They are VIP's too*" (Chippindale, 2022). Although a fashion show running late is not uncommon in which attendees accept, as Chippindale clearly explains, the same rules do not apply when you're dealing with online communities.

Figure 4-11a. *Tommy Hilfiger autumn/winter 2022/2023 fashion show*

Figure 4-11b. *Tommy Factory Roblox digital collection*

Figure 4-11c. *Tommy Factory Roblox digital outfit*

Figure 4-11d. *Tommy Factory AR experience*

Multiverse or metaverse marketing is still in its infancy within fashion, predominantly because brands are still getting their heads around the concept, but in the future, such digital campaigns will be a lot easier to build. Seelig believes that metaverse building will be akin to how building an e-commerce store is at present on plug-and-play e-commerce store builders (think Shopify, etc.). This will take another 10 to 20 years to perfect, as it did with e-commerce stores, but brands must prepare now to enter the space.

4.4. Marketing Sustainability and Circularity Tech

There's no hiding the fact that fashion is one of the most polluting industries in the world. Depending on what study you're reading, the industry fluctuates between top ten places but is always there, nonetheless. As explored in the previous chapter, technology and innovations can help the industry work toward a more sustainable future in a variety of areas including reducing carbon emissions, waste management, increasing product longevity, and more.

In response to climate change, consumer demands for more sustainable products and initiatives and enforced legislations; brands are deploying tech at speed to work toward a greener future. The Ellen MacArthur Foundation predicts that brands could *"unlock a USD 560 billion economic opportunity"* (2023) by implementing circular systems into their businesses, which sounds great. However, are brands integrating such systems because they care, or are they marketing such initiatives for clout and monetary gain? In essence greenwashing. Fashion Revolution, a nonprofit organization tackling societal and environmental industry issues, defines greenwashing: *"greenwashing is when brands, corporations, organizations or governments co-opt sustainability narratives to portray an environmentally responsible image without sufficiently responsible action"* (2023). Sustainability is such a large scope, so we'll focus on circularity for this section. Example technologies include the following: Table 4-2.

Table 4-2. *Technologies enable circular fashion*

Circular System Activity	Description and Technologies	Example Companies
Rental	Platforms that enable either mono-brand rentals or multi-brand rentals, B2C, B2B, or C2C	Rent the Runway, By Rotation, Lizee, Nuuly
Repair	Repair services delivered through online and digital channels. B2B or B2C	Tilli, Clothes Doctor, The Cobblers, Save Your Wardrobe, Archive
Resale	Platforms enabling preloved fashion to be resold including C2C, B2B white label, and B2C	Reflaunt, By Rotation, Vestiaire Collective, Depop, BizB, Vinted, thredUP, The RealReal, Archive
Recycling/ Regeneration/ Upcycling	Hardware solutions recycling products, or digital platforms managing the process	Resortecs, Finds, Save Your Wardrobe, Queen of Raw: Materia MX

Each of the different types of circular system activities requires a different approach when being marketed and can be powerful tools for communicating to the consumer tangible actions that a company is taking toward sustainability or circularity. Connor Hill, CEO of circular strategies consultancy Inspire Circular, notes that *"resale and repair are going to be more low hanging fruits for them [the brands] because the consumer is already in that mindset. However, circularity's starting point should be to increase the recycled content of a product as much as possible, therefore increasing durability and longevity to make the product last longer"* (2023).

4.4.1. Own-Brand Resale Platforms

thredUP, a popular marketplace for preloved fashion serving North America, releases an annual report on the resale and secondhand clothing market to highlight the impact such platforms have. According to the 2023 report, there was a 3.4× increase in the number of retailers launching their own-brand resale platforms with H&M having the highest number (approximately 30,000 items) of secondhand clothing listings on their platform at the time of writing this book. From a marketing perspective, such program launches have allowed brands to benefit from an increase in brand loyalty (thredUP, 2023), meaning such activations do contribute significantly to sustainability-led marketing campaigns. The tools we're about to discuss serve such marketing campaigns, and without them, many campaigns would ring hollow. Therefore, greenwashing.

White label technologies (a technology that is developed by a third-party provider and is rebranded by another user or client to pass off as their own) such as Reflaunt's branded recommerce platform and concierge resale service enable any fashion brand to launch their own version of a preloved fashion website. This plug-and-play solution lowers the barrier for execution and from a marketing perspective can be activated at speed, in which Reflaunt's clients such as Balenciaga and Altuzarra have used to their advantage.

From a technical perspective, Reflaunt's proprietary technology includes hardware and infrastructure that enables brands to easily link to marketplaces, ensuring that customers get a seamless customer journey. Customers can easily list their previously purchased items back on the brand's resale website, authenticated by digital IDs (as discussed in Chapter 3) and thus closing the loop. The platform's product assortment feature also ensures that pages on the resale platform are curated and marketed into relevant collections for new customers to purchase from. This entire back-end infrastructure enables brands and customers to market and sell preloved items with ease.

Reflaunt does a lot of the heavy lifting on behalf of the brand and customer, whereas a similar solution by Archive integrates into the brand's experience by offering a white label peer-to-peer resale offering and placing an emphasis more on the customer. Technical features include proprietary warehouse management systems specifically designed for resale items and a retail app that enables brands to market and execute effectively in-store take-back programs. Therefore, the experience of resale can be tackled and implemented from multiple angles depending on the brand's objectives. However, many own-brand resale platforms are still a minor project alongside the fashion brands' main business.

We looked at some of the own-brand resale platforms that have launched in recent years, and at large they still feel as though they are still separate, or a check box exercise. We'll dig a bit deeper as to why this is. Patagonia, *the* outdoor clothing brand known for its environmental values, launched their "Worn Wear" program in 2013 as part of a marketing campaign to counterbalance the usual fashion week schedule. Primarily offline activity, the dedicated web platform outside of the main e-commerce website launched in 2017 with resale and repair activities (Figure 4-12a). Although we love the initiative and it certainly supports sustainability and circularity, as of the writing of this section, spring 2023, there are only approximately 9200 products for sale on their website across men's and women's.

Considering that the program has been in existence for ten years, the number of products is very low. This could be in part because the online resale marketplace is currently only available in the United States and the experience currently does not seem that favorable for the customer considering the completely separate customer experience from the main Patagonia website (Figure 4-12a), high barrier for products to be accepted for resale, and the low store credit offered for accepted goods. Bearing in mind that Patagonia still places a two to three times markup on the items deemed suitable for resale, there seems to be a disconnect between people, planet, and profit.

Figure 4-12a. *Worn Wear stand-alone resale website*

Figure 4-12b. *Sandro resale website, May 2023*

Similarly in Europe, French premium brand Sandro launched their own-brand resale website by utilizing Archive in 2022 (Figure 4-12b). From Peter's experience of the men's section of the website, offering only three pages' worth of product doesn't make a compelling offering or experience.

Thus, unlikely to return to the resale site anytime soon and left feeling with the notion of a brand check box exercise being activated.

It makes sense that more brands are wanting to launch their own versions of a circular activation, as third-party platforms such as Vinted, Depop, and Vestiaire Collective have taken large chunks of the market share that they could have capitalized on – capitalized meaning financially, brand image and customer retention, or ownership on own-brand products. Hill notes for brands to launch own-brand circular activations, considerable financial investment as well as a longer-term strategy over ten years vs. one or two years is required. Additionally, such activations need to have a strong MVP to be fully integrated into the core business proposition, but because of the investment and longer timeline to see ROI, projects are often downplayed.

> *"There's no consistency as to who or which department initiates the circular strategy. It could be executives, product, or innovation departments depending on the activation required. There is no consistency and therefore no consistent way of marketing." (Hill, 2023)*

4.4.2. The Circularity Ingredients

Going back to greenwashing, this will be increasingly more difficult as new laws and technologies advance. We mentioned earlier in Chapter 3 the AGEC law in regard to transparency and traceability, but of course it extends far beyond that. Otherwise known as the anti-waste law working toward a circular economy, passed in 2020, it was created to ensure that companies operating in France comply with dealing with their products accordingly: eco-design of products, responsible consumption, extension of shelf life, and recycling of products and waste. Therefore, elements such as labeling products with the environmental footprint or recycled materials content need to be clearly displayed and understandable. The articles of the law can be found on the French government website: `www.legifrance.gouv.fr`.

Such laws are drastically paving the way for new technologies to enable the execution of such legislations. Once France shows what has or hasn't worked with the AGEC law; it'll provide a blueprint for the rest of the European Union states and hopefully the rest of the world. Regardless of if a law is in place or not, brands can still effectively market circular and sustainable activations. Hill (2023) believes that there are eight different ingredients needed to be truly circular:

1. Materials: Recycled, regenerative, or renewable content that is durable. Brands such as these to market clearly what their products are made from.

2. Durability and longevity: Messaging that encourages consumers to utilize their products longer (providing that a brand's products can actually last longer).

3. Commercial and design of product: How are you making it seasonless? Is the product multifunctional, etc.? Utility in different use cases (e.g., gym to socializing) is important for reducing overconsumption.

4. Production: Reducing and recycling waste. Brands need to utilize and market circular or more sustainable production methods such as less fabric offcuts and wastage, or clean dyeing.

5. Slow(er) fashion: Producing closer to the release date to avoid deeply discounted sales or offering made-to-order products.

6. Extended life: Offering and clearly marketing services to make products last longer like care and repair (i.e., Clothes Doctor).

7. Care instructions online: Content leading to additional circular services such as sending T-shirts back to get them white again.

8. Sorting at end of life: Providing ways for customers to consciously place their preloved fashion back into the circular system. Think resale (such as Worn Wear) and recycling programs that are then managed by systems such as Finds.

What we can see from the list of ingredients is that no one technology or initiative can make fashion truly circular and tick all of these ingredients. The problem is that most fashion technologies trying to implement circularity are doing so within a well-established linear system (as shown at the start of this book). Hill (2023) notes that it's more about the "nudge effects" that are required:

"Circularity is all about keeping the same thing for longer, and that goes against the linear capitalist model of 'make more, sell more, and more profit.' However, circularity and growth can happen together. Key questions are: how can you continue to grow your business in a more resource light way? How do you create revenue from those middle services [like ingredients 7 & 8]? Brands can make money from the services in the middle and still achieve growth. Therefore, it's an educational journey and uses lots of different case studies to decide on the best circular practices."

For brands not to have sustainability campaigns seem like frivolous activations; it's about the longer-term view. For example, the Lablaco and Circular Fashion Summit do require their event (paying) partners to commit to a minimum of 12-months' worth of activity and not just for marketing visibility during the three- or four-day event. The Galeries Lafayette offline in-store campaign discussed in Section 4.2 is an example. However, it is still opaque as to how much impact such an activation made toward the greenwashing issue. Ultimately, consumers are still driven by value when making purchases, even if sustainability is high on the agenda, especially for Generation Z (thredUP, 2023). This causes growth bugbears for circular and sustainability tech of their own, as seen by luxury authenticated-goods resale platform The RealReal and their threat of bankruptcy in 2022 followed by discontinuation of their beauty category in 2023.

4.5. Chapter Summary

What we can learn from this chapter:

- Showcasing products through technologies such as VR and AR is not only a way to push sales but actually there is importance in simply increasing the time that a customer spends on the brand's website or virtual space.

- It's still difficult for some tech companies to convince brands to change the way they showcase their products from the traditional imagery on their website; however, those open to the idea have seen some increase in customer engagement

- Purposes of these more visual technologies are slightly different to when AI is used as the data received from it differs (e.g., numeric data vs. visualization of the items being showcased).

Have you given virtual worlds and try-ons a go? Here are some to try on (pun intended). To access links, use the QR code from the beginning of the book.

Table 4-3. *List of virtual worlds & try-ons*

Source	Access	Brand	Try-On Items
DressX	Smartphone	Multiple	Garments
SnapChat Lenses	Smartphone	Gucci and Farfetch	Sneakers
YSL website	All devices	YSL Beauty	Make-up
Lablaco	Oculus Quest	Various designers	Clothing
Wanna Kicks & Wear	Smartphone	Multiple	Footwear, accessories, clothing
Zero10	Smartphone	Multiple	Clothing and handbags

CHAPTER 5

Smart Retail and Stores of the Future

5.1. Redesigning Physical Shopping Experience

Online shopping is a popular form of retail for the fashion industry; however, the physical store is still dominating this last phase. According to Statista, 69.8% of purchases in the fashion industry in the Americas are still made via physical shopping compared to online (Statista, 2023). This means that the shopping journey is one of the most crucial to consider transforming when concerning fashion technologies. The standard format of the physical shopping experience typically runs in this order:

1. Browse in between the aisles and rails.

2. Pick up desired items from the shelves and rails.

3. If needed, physically try on the garments or shoes, etc., in the fitting rooms/areas.

4. Then queue up to pay at the till.

At each of these points, there are multiple opportunities to modify the experience for the customers to experience it differently in terms of time-saving, or more personalization with tools such as size recommendations. Through these, the shop floor format is redesigned.

We saw in Chapter 4 that one side of this new physical experience in-store, such as implementing VR installations, works for marketing efforts while not completely changing the physical shopping experience itself. In this section, we will see that the alternative step is to completely transform the shopping journey itself at either of the parts listed previously.

There are various startups who have had the chance to implement their solutions into fashion stores. While some do this with the purpose of helping the brands increase their sales, others aim to improve customer satisfaction. The common factor between them all is that brands simply need to see results such as in-store engagements and sales to validate their decision of adopting this technology. As with any business, key performance indicators can help to measure this impact of adopting technology including monitoring customer buying habits during their shopping.

5.1.1. Perfecting Fit with In-Store Body Scanning

The fit of a fashion product is one of the key factors of how well it will sell. Whether it be in-store or online shopping, one key driver for customers to purchase a product or not depends on how well it fits their body. Who wants an ill-fitting garment that makes you look like you got dressed in the dark right? For retailers, the fit and sizing are an important element to communicate and get right for the customer as it could mean lost revenue, product returns, and reduced profit margins if not done correctly. In a study conducted by IMRG (The UK Ecommerce Association) and Rebound, a company that deals with online returns on behalf of companies, clothing is the highest product category for returns with some companies having a return rate of up to 45% (IMRG & Rebound, 2022).

In-store, although customers can try on products before purchase, it can be just as confusing for some as every brand has their own sizing and fit. There is no universal industry standard. Coupled with other factors such as geographical location, customers may not know their sizing for that specific brand, which may result in unpurchased items or body type-to-fit mismatch. Technology is slowly helping to solve the fit and sizing issues for retailers with tools such as virtual try-on through smartphones or magic mirrors, 3D body scanners, and fit analytics as explored in previous chapters. However, many of these solutions are yet to be deployed at scale or industry-wide, meaning that there're still a lot of opportunities to be had.

There are a variety of elements that can be improved by the help of technologies in this scenario, including sizing. If you are a female and reading this, you may be wearing the wrong bra – in terms of size that is. This is according to Haniff Brown who has been establishing his sizing startup solution, FIT:MATCH.ai, and caught the eyes of brands such as Rihanna's Savage X Fenty to implement into their physical fitting rooms. The brand already embraces inclusivity from a wide range of sizes they offer for their products to the diverse models in their marketing campaigns so it only made sense for them to implement a tech solution that would help reinforce this. Placing the FIT:MATCH.ai Fit Xperience tool in the physical fitting rooms means that the customer can have a more accurate size and style recommendation of their lingerie – supporting the sentiment of the brand having a variety of products fit for all shapes and sizes.

This is how the solution works:

1. Enter into the fitting room and undress into an unpadded, unlined bra and leggings for accuracy.

2. Get scanned within three seconds using the Fit Xperience tool in the changing room (Figure 5-1a).

3. Receive product match recommendations in your best-fitting sizes across bra styles.

4. Purchase the bra at the till.

Figure 5-1a. *Savage X Fenty fitting room with the Fit Xperience tool*

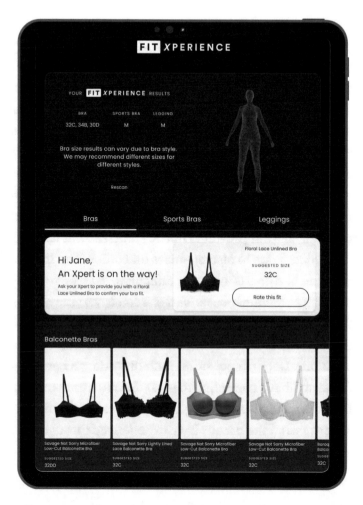

Figure 5-1b. *Screenshot of FIT:MATCH.ai measuring and analyzing breast shape and recommending size per style according to discrepancies*

FIT:MATCH.ai matches the customers to the right product sizes as accurately as possible through Apple's LiDAR tools. After creating the digital version of the customer, an analysis is done to not only recommend the size according to the measurements but also according to the shape as shown in Figure 5-1b. Not only does this limit the physical contact between a customer and shopping assistant/fitting room assistant, but it also provides 93% accuracy (Littleton, 2023) with its recommendations compared to the traditional measuring tape that could produce discrepancies when used incorrectly. Humans are naturally different from each other in terms of body types; therefore, putting each person in a box according to their size has proven to not be sufficient when shapes need to also be considered due to discrepancies that differ from the standard clothing fit. Some body parts are more difficult to categorize by sizes than others, such as female breasts with extremely varying shapes. This is why FIT:MATCH.ai has focused their solution on lingerie to allow the discrepancies of the varying shapes to be taken into account during the recommendations. Department stores including Macy's have also adopted FIT:MATCH.ai and have continued to push this into more branches across the United States, which is a good sign of the value the solution is bringing. The following are what the brands have experienced through offering this to their customers in store:

- Conversion rate is at **6x**.

- Returning **80%** less.

- Have **20–30%** higher average order values.

- Confident in their recommended size.

- **99%** of those who scan no longer bracket shop (buy multiple sizes).

- **2x** more likely to join the brand's loyalty program.

- Accounting for **25%** of the Gross Merchandise Value for bras.

When researching the overall shopping experiences that validate these types of solutions, studied shoppers spent on average one to three hours on shopping, including trying on items in the fitting rooms in pursuit of their desired fashion items, and still may walk out with a purchase that fits them (Damir Anic et al., 2018). This is why a solution like this is necessary and can also save a lot of time that would usually be spent trying on and comparing the same items in multiple sizes. There are customers who don't mind spending time browsing around a physical store, while others prefer a quicker in and out type of shopping. In this case, interacting with marketing-focused technologies such as those described in Chapter 4 would be less appealing for brands compared to these more physical solutions when their aim is to push metrics in relation to sales. Cutting down the time spent shopping, or in this case avoiding trying on clothes in multiple sizes, in a store is one way that the customers benefit from this and makes it easier to make a purchase without potential disruptions from ill-fitting garments in the fitting room along the way.

Let's take this measurement concept deeper into another specific body part: the foot. When considering your shoe size, how often have you measured your foot as opposed to simply matching with whichever shoe appeared to fit? Most of the time we do the latter and can often even be in between sizes. This mixed with shoe sizes, styles, and customer foot shapes differing in every store makes it rather a gamble each time we purchase footwear, especially online.

The physical store allows you to tangibly try on shoes while online would not. Extending the ability to scan the foot first before entering the physical store is another way to link the fitting technologies with the physical shopping experience which is what solutions such as Shoefitr focus on. Leaving the house with the understanding of your foot measurements as opposed to your shoe size only can be the step further to finding a better fit when physically shopping. While this may not completely eradicate the "trying on" experience in store, it is one of the solutions that take into account discrepancies between what stores are offering as standard sizes vs. the realities of how different each customer's feet and, in the case of FIT:MATCH.ai, breasts are.

When looking beyond the main purposes of these technologies (reduce returns and transform the overall shopping experience), the other parts of the supply chain can also use this data as a starting point to rethinking the standard sizes and styles currently offered by the brands.

5.1.2. Designing a Shopping Journey Around Fit

3D body scanning, as we've seen with FIT:MATCH.ai, is the bearer of all body measurement truth. It's a highly accurate way of obtaining body measurements instantly. We've scanned ourselves several times using a 3D body scanner (Figure 5-2b), and it is undoubtedly the best way to see yourself in a revealing yet accurate way. Many retailers are now offering in-store body scanning as part of the in-store customer experience to close the gap between a customer's body size and shape and the product fit of the brand. Decathlon, the French sporting goods retailer, is one example of a retailer that is experimenting with in-store body scanning by partnering with a fit and sizing company, Treedy's. Treedy's is a company that aims to *"understand what makes everyone unique by their morphology and do it right for it for everyone"* as David Francotte (2023), CEO, tells us. Treedy's creates digital twins of the customer via 3D body scanning and is then able to recommend the best size for that user via the app or in-store screen, similar to what we saw with FIT:MATCH.ai.

In-store body scanning is still in its experimental phase, as the partnership between Decathlon and Treedy's illustrates (Figure 5-2a). The retailer approached the company without a brief in terms of how to design or deploy the in-store experience but knew that they wanted to deploy an accurate measuring system that allows them to understand the customer better. In turn, they intend to use this information to innovate on products and produce in a more responsible way. At the time of this book being published, the Treedy's solution is installed at three Decathlon locations in different countries, the largest being an 8,500-square-meter store located in Madrid, Spain. For a store of this size, the scanner may get lost in the customer journey, but results show that 2% of all in-store visitors are spontaneously scanning themselves. The scans are then resulting in 45% of users creating a member's accounts and 97% utilizing the size advice that is given to them at the time of scanning. This demonstrates in-store scanning can have a positive impact for both retailer and consumer.

Although the Decathlon case study shows positive results, accuracy and development of the physical equipment and digital solution took time to achieve. David and his team spent 1.5 years to perfect a scanner that could scale, and then a further 3.5 years to build the full solution. This illustrates why it's so difficult to perfect fit and size across the fashion industry – it's not a quick turnaround. *"But the first step is to find the right partners like we did with Decathlon. That's what took us at least a year and a half to start discussing the solution we had with customers, with brands. That being said, I believe that today the whole industry is waking up"* (Francotte, 2023). Although Decathlon is a retailer, the company also takes a tech forward approach, which is vital for solutions like Treedy's to be adopted.

Technically, Treedy's system started with a denoising algorithm (an algorithm that removes noise (random and undesired variations of image aspects such as brightness) from graphics and renders to improve the quality of the final output), which is layered with their patented technology, Nakednet. Nakednet is an AI system that has been trained with over 900,000 data points from human scans. By utilizing the data gathered, the company can build out a full picture of the consumers' morphology and integrate it into their app called "Landmarkpoint." The app utilizes 250 points on the body to offer sizing advice once a user has completed a body scan. The points are interchangeable and modifiable depending on the needs of the retailer that Treedy's is working with. David expects that the Treedy's solution should help retailers see over 20% reduction in returns.

Aside from returns, other benefits of such technology include reduction in measurement costs, for example, for retailers with a tailoring service. Treedy's scanner was able to scan and process 100 people in eight hours, meaning faster production turnaround times. Treedy's fit and size solution can also be elaborated into other avenues including the following:

1. Morphological data analysis per market segment.

2. Parametric clothing. An automated tech pack from the output measurements to allow made-to-order at scale.

3. Heatmap visualization, allowing customers to determine the comfort of any garment.

4. Tech-pack analysis to automatically determine the intended body type of any item.

Ultimately the notion of body scanning is to sell recommended products that are available in-store or online in an experience that is personalized to the customer (Figure 5-2c). Other customers of Treedy's include Nike, Zalando, and Amazon, which the latter acquired a similar company "Body Labs" in 2017 to bolster its understanding of the human body.

Figure 5-2a. *Treedy's body scanner in-store setup located in Rennes, France*

Figure 5-2b. *Treedy's body scanner machine*

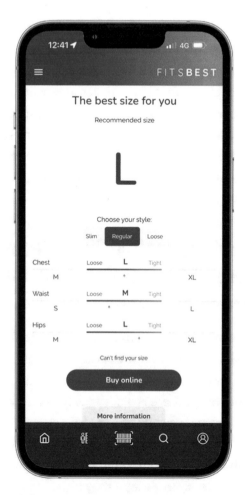

Figure 5-2c. *Treedy's size recommendation app*

5.1.3. End of the Shopping Journey

Once the items have been selected and it is time to head to the till to make the purchase, there can often be a long queue in the way. This waiting period can put customers off, and 63% of the surveyed consumers by Fashion United mentioned that they would abandon the purchase altogether in these scenarios (Fashion United, 2014). This is one of the reasons why many customers would avoid physically shopping in the first place. Fortunately, there are solutions that focus on this part of the shopping journey specifically to accelerate the process including MishiPay. This is a scale-up that has driven the link between smartphones and the physical store to purchase items without queuing up, which has been made possible through two features: (1) using the phone as a quick checkout system without the need of a till in the store and (2) self-checkout kiosks that do not require the usual manual scanning but can recognize all items almost instantly through RFID.

5.1.4. Insider Perspective: Transforming the Physical Store Checkout Systems. Interview with Mustafa Khanwala, Founder and CEO at MishiPay

VR: How did you get into retail tech and what are the problems that you see in the industry that led you to develop the queue-less payment solution?

MK: I had the idea after I waited 20 minutes in a line just to buy a coke. And I thought "surely there is a better way to check out." It made a lot of sense that you can use your phone to do everything else so why not for shopping, right? Why can't we just scan the barcode, pay on our phone, and leave the store? And so, I started looking into it and I saw a lot of retailers are facing the same issues – they must make their stores more efficient while they improve the customer experience and increase their sales, so it was a double issue, and we were determined to help solve it.

VR: So how did you manage to convince the investors and potential clients that this is the future?

MK: At first, they were like, "yeah, I get it – I wouldn't want to wait in the line myself," but at the same time were afraid of the gamble it would be to be an early investor or adopter. The solution tackles inside the store, which was seen as being harder to integrate as it meant that you must deal with the operations, theft prevention, and more. It's harder than plugging a few lines of code to a website.

First, retail tech became exciting and sexy as you started seeing Amazon Go type of projects launch. Then, there was a big crash during the pandemic where all stores had to shut down. These stores could not rehire the same number of staff due to all the impacts, which meant that they had to look at tech to help them out.

In 2016, we were selling only an RFID solution, but suddenly this had to change. It now had to be a solution available to all retailers regardless of their RFID status. Self-checkout was already there for brands such as Zara at this point so now we had to change it up with other benefits.

VR: What is the technology that is powering the two solutions?

MK: The first element is the integration into the brands' back-end. We must get the details of the items such as name, price, images, descriptions to register it to the app. This links with all transactions made back into the retailer's system. There are approximately seven systems that we integrate in the back end, synchronize them in real time, and provide the front end on iOS, Android, and web.

The second element is regarding the scanning at the self-checkout kiosk. It's an Android-based system right on the tablets. We have two main hardware providers: Zebra and Elo.

Lastly, our trust engine is there for theft prevention so the stores that use RFID can simply have them deactivated upon purchase to stop the alarms from being set off.

All of these not only help the brands front-on but through those, they can also view the transactions, scanning data, refunds, and analytics for their own analyses while making the self-checkout simpler.

VR: When focusing on your pilots and your fashion clients, what made them approach you?

MK: They simply want to make more money in-store, and to achieve this, they need to limit the customer frustrations as much as possible. As a customer in a store, if you really love that T-shirt, you will wait in line and get it, but the long queues may deter you from coming back next time. We've seen that we've been able to increase the basket value up 25 to 35%

because more time can be spent browsing rather than queuing up. We have seen this with lifestyle brands like Flying Tiger, who has subsequently rolled out the solution to across the UK because of the pilot success.

We also have an NPS (net promoter score) over 72 in all our fashion stores. We also give the customer the ability to rate us out of five, and our rating is over 4.85. This validates the satisfaction of the users.

VR: What's next for MishiPay?

MK: This year [2023] we're looking to have 1,000,000 transactions per month. We are currently at 120,000 per month. We are also looking to get to $100 million in ARR within the next three years and just be known as the dominant method of self-checkout in stores across multiple cities.

Figure 5-3. *Scanning barcode using the MishiPay app as mode of checkout in store*

5.2. Redesigning the Online Experience

5.2.1. Virtual Try-On with Filters

For solutions already explored in this book, including Treedy's, Shoefitr, and other scanning solutions, the avatars or digital twins of the customers are the focus of the visual representation of the data collected according to their morphology. Other solutions have prioritized the live display of the customer on their phone or on screens instead without the measurements. This is available in both "the living room" context as well as in stores. The key to the success of this type of virtual try-on is to focus on the purpose of implementation of the technology and the best way it serves the brand.

As previously discovered in Section 4.1.1 and the previous section, there is still no "one size fits all" solution that focuses on both virtual try-on and body scanning together. This keeps the gap between the measurements and visual representation of a product and drives different use cases for either of them separately. Out of all of the solutions that we have researched, there is still yet a solution that accurately combines both elements; we can see that brands are adopting only one solution out of the two that best caters to their brand values or business objectives. If the brand isn't after a solution that gratifies the need for (almost) perfect fitting with measurements from customer body scans, then they are after simply enhancing the customer experience and increasing dwell time. This is the case for brands who have worked with Wanna, a virtual try-on solution (VTO) that has been acquired by Farfetch.

Figure 5-4a. *Wanna online platform*

They have worked on multiple platforms from a B2C as well as B2B perspective via Snapchat and on the websites of the brands, providing a virtual try-on tool for the products being sold. Similarly to what we have seen in Section 4.1.2, this can be seen as a marketing tool; however, when embedded in the online retail experience, it can be a powerful tool for visualizing the potential fit of the items on the customers as opposed to providing measurements. During one of the integrations sampled during a two-week period, Wanna found that "*AR virtual try-on functionality drove an increase in visits by +47%, add to bag visits by +22%, and add to wish list visits by +81% vs similar products (watches) with a similar price point that did not have the AR virtual try-on function turned on [on the FARFETCH site]*" (Wanna, 2022).

Figure 5-4b. *Von digitally wearing the virtual watch by Wanna*

Figure 5-4c. *Von trying on digital sneakers by Wanna*

Customers are still unable to experience live virtual try-on with a tactile element as it obviously is not physical. There is no physical contact with the products as it is specifically "trying on virtually." The gratifying feeling of the dress hugging you the right way or the blazer sitting correctly on you is unmatched for the virtual try-on solution as it's not currently possible to tangibly interact with the digital projections. This would be linked to some of the challenges expressed by Wanna during their sampling when trying but not being able to fully:

- Increase conversion rate above benchmark.

- Increase revenue from seasonal sneaker full-price sales.

However, customers show that they still have a growing appetite for this solution as when concerning retail, the multinational e-commerce company Shopify saw a 94% conversion rate on their merchants who use 3D content, AR virtual try-ons, or AR style showrooms (Shopify, 2023). Perhaps these technologies are meant to synergize between each other as one app. A scanner and a virtual try-on next to it to get a full scope of the potential that these technologies have to offer to help make purchasing choices.

5.2.2. Fitting Fashion Tech to Diverse Body Types

Fashion brands and tech experts who join forces for the stated collaborations generally tend to stick to a standard body type when putting fashion technology to practice. An issue that is already prevalent in the industry from the traditional sizing charts that don't consider plus sizes to the shopping journeys that typically aren't the most accessible for disabled shoppers. According to Statista, New York, London, Paris, and Milan fall/winter 2023 season catwalks had "almost all of the 9,000+ looks exhibited in U.S. sizes 0 to 4. Only 0.6 percent of the looks were in [U.S.]

sizes 14 and over" (Statista, 2023). When specifically looking at the use of fashion technologies such as AR and AI virtual try-ons, one can argue that there is flexibility for plus size users where the scanning would not discriminate. However, if the clothing remains to be unavailable in those sizes, there continues to be a mismatch between what is being offered by brands vs. the customer needs. This would result in the need for matching of the concerned technologies to the appropriate brands. In this case, an AI digital size recommendation solution would be appropriate for a brand that offers various sizes beyond the US size 12, "which is traditionally the largest size many clothing retailers offer" (Statista 2023).

While the sizing issue remains an important issue for brands to consider, the term "body types" extends to the varying abilities that also exist, which also need attention. There are 1.3 billion disabled people in the world, making that 1 in 6 of the population (World Health Organization 2023) that needs clothing and fashion products that are more accessible than the minute buttons on shirt cuffs or the extremely tight skinny jeans that are already difficult to put on without a disability. While disabled people remain a minority of the population, this number is still relatively large, and the adaptive apparel market is estimated at a value of USD 348.81 billion by 2024 (Statista 2022), meaning a demand for inclusive products and shopping experiences. This is where the traditional ways of "doing fashion" continue to exclude another group of customers even if it may not be intentional. There are only a handful of mainstream fashion brands dedicatedly offering adaptive fashion lines including Tommy Hilfiger and Zappos along with the smaller fashion brands like Von Ruz by Von.

Adaptive fashion is still limited with the technologies explored to match. If we look at the virtual try-on or body scanning technologies that we have covered, the one thing that is common is the way something is detected on the screens/phones to utilize these technologies. In this case, the bodies that are expected to use these virtual try-ons, etc., are the typical ones with all limbs, ability to stand and change the posture, and so on, which disabled bodies, according to their abilities, may not be able to do. While trying on virtual garments such as jackets, automatically there are two sleeves that appear on the screen simultaneously, the virtual sneakers generally are showcased with two feet while the user may not have all limbs.

While some technologies give room for the seated body in an indirect way, for example, virtual worlds in VR and virtual try-on of sneakers on smartphones and other garments that only require certain parts of the body as opposed to the whole body in a certain manner, these appear to be subconsciously inclusive efforts. The question is, is inclusivity a priority when developing or adopting the technologies discussed? When looking past the interactive shopping experiences that require the user to be visible on the smartphone or in-store AR screens, the virtual worlds that require avatars also currently miss the mark. Missing limbs or seated positions are "not common options in many avatar platforms" (Mack et al. 2023), besides a few companies like Meta that recently launched a new wave of varying avatars and inclusive features.

Von having worked on her own fashion brand that is inclusive of people with disabilities, it is no surprise to see that the lack of inclusivity has extended to the fashion technology side of the industry. This is a problem that the industry appears to be speaking about a lot, with articles released on this topic consecutively, without enough action to combat the issue and let it actually stick. Sure, we have had some disabled models featured in some fashion brand campaigns as well as on the front of Vogue for the first time in the Spring 2023 issue; however, what are the brands selling or doing to continue this throughout the rest of the value chain? For example, if we rewind back to the start of the design phase, research into varying abilities for more inclusive styles is not part of the traditional process and reinforces what is seen at retail stage, offering of standardized products. Linking this with what fashion technologies currently have to offer, "when excluded from the design process, people with disabilities can be left feeling neglected and invisible as virtual worlds become more commonplace" (Mack et al. 2023). An example where representation is required in the virtual world as these technologies continue to develop and become normalized platforms for fashion retail.

Microsoft has been one of the few technology companies to fully dedicate departments of their workforce to developing genuinely inclusive products and campaigns. These are the types of companies with these kinds of values that need to have a push when creating more inclusive fashion technology solutions. The inclusive gaming controllers developed by Microsoft are an example of how existing products can adopt new features to make them easier to use from an overall practical standpoint. When using the technologies mentioned, representation is important, but usability is also key to consider the different abilities that the users may have. "Digital services could be both beneficial and problematic to disabled people depending on their needs, their access to digital services and their ability to use them" (Office for National Statistics 2022).

The products currently being marketed and sold through the technologies discussed in this book are already predominantly standardized and not inclusive of different body types, which leads to less demand for the technologies being adopted by these same brands to be inclusive also. What happens when we try to do it the other way round where someone with an atypical body type uses these technologies? Inclusivity in fashion remains untapped, but when specifically looking into this synergy with technology, opportunities open up for more innovation that can enhance inclusive experience for different users. Not just at the retail stage but the influence can spread across the whole supply chain.

Table 5-1. *Table with recommendations for further inclusivity in fashion tech*

Fashion technology	Elements to focus on per tool	Recommendation
AR virtual try-on	– Body analysis	Develop tech that allows the different body types to be dressed accordingly (e.g., AR that can detect different body types to adapt the items accordingly. This would depend on the offering of each brand)
VR virtual world shopping	– Avatars – The VR goggles used	Include avatars that have different body types and other social signals
AI body scanning	– Body analysis	Develop tech or improve machine learning that can analyze different body types (e.g., detect any missing limbs). Integrations likes these may require further advancements of the technology

Table 5-1 shows recommendations on how to make a more inclusive shopping experience.

5.2.3. Instant Fashion at a Click

Once upon a time when e-commerce exploded in the late 2000s, it was touted that online retail would cannibalize offline retail in growth and market share. That obviously hasn't happened, aided by the redesign of the retail format and shopping experience as explored at the start of this chapter. However, online fashion retail still accounts for 21% to 30% of fashion transactions globally, with China and North America being the top two markets, and is expected to be worth over USD 1.2 trillion by 2027 (Statista, 2023). *Instant.* This is the keyword synonymous with e-commerce and is driving consumers to shop online, and online is synonymous with technology, digital, and innovation.

The Fourth Industrial Revolution, as explored in Chapter 1, the blurring of physical and digital spheres, encapsulates where online retailing could be taking us. One example of this being explored is the "see now, buy now" business model introduced by Tommy Hilfiger in 2016 and later followed suit by brands like Burberry and Rebecca Minkoff. See now, buy now means that pieces of the brands' collections are available for purchase as soon as they are debuted on the catwalk. The strategy behind the model is to bring showcase and retail calendars closer together to cater to consumers penchant for instant fashion, but also to address merchandising issues so that in-demand products would sell quicker, thus reducing overproduction.

To make "see now, buy now" happen, technologies such as shoppable live streams and videos of catwalk shows are deployed. Smartzer, a company that deploys such technology, has seen positive results across a variety of brands including their campaigns with Adidas that have seen up to 62% engagement rate and 20% click-through rate. In some cases, the return on investment (ROI) has seen a multiple of 8× (Smartzer, 2023), showing that fashion immediacy is real. However, see now, buy now hasn't been widely adopted and is quite often referred to as a marketing trick rather than a real change in industrial and retail processes. Supply chain and logistics are two of the reasons why it's so difficult to implement: the current system is very difficult to change, but many fashion executives believe that it is a top priority focus: "*more than half of fashion executives believe supply chain disruptions will be one of the top factors impacting growth of the global economy in 2023*" (Business of Fashion, 2022). What this means for instant fashion at a click is that the industry can currently only work in advance when it comes to production, as opposed to on-demand as we explored in Chapter 3.

5.2.4. The Last Mile

The final phase of the journey of an online purchase from warehouse to the customer is called "the last mile." It is historically the most expensive, logistically difficult, and environmentally unfriendly part of the online retail experience that fashion brands must figure out. It can be a purchase decision deal breaker for many customers and thus is important to address. For example, Gen Z consumers who are drivers of instant gratification care more about the speed of delivery that an online retailer offers over other generations (Retail Economics, 2019), yet at the same time want to know more about the carbon footprint that said deliveries produce as a result. However, they feel that many online retailers are not transparent enough about their delivery options to make an informed decision. Online retailers could address this by being more transparent about delivery impact at the online checkout and ultimately offer sustainable delivery solutions that would greatly influence their purchasing decision (Unidays & Zendify, 2022).

Last mile technology, the term used to describe technologies that collectively improve the last mile, could be deployed to streamline logistics operations, reduce costs, and improve the online customer experience during the final delivery phase. Such technologies include drones, autonomous delivery vehicles (ADV), and robots from a physical perspective and logistics management platforms from the software side. Each one of these elements utilizes data, analytics, and AI to get the delivery to the customer in the best way possible. Fashion is yet to adopt many of the technologies as they are not yet scalable or authorized by local governments; however, companies such as Amazon are trialing drone delivery with Amazon Air in the United States for small essential packages. For ADV and robots, the large supermarkets are conducting trials globally to understand what a fully automated delivery service may look like. Once these cases have been proven, then fashion will adopt.

Although these technologies are still nascent, instant fashion is available using the current infrastructure. Farfetch is one online retailer that offers 90-minute delivery service. Known for their prowess on logistics and global network management, they partner with tech providers such as Sorted and ParcelLab to consolidate their logistics network to enable such a retail promise. With fashion being so easy to purchase instantaneously, this also causes many online returns since for consumers, it is that easy to return items too. In the UK, clothing is the most returned product category, and the average return rate for online fashion retail is around 30% (Statista 2023). This is a huge problem for the industry that many tech companies are trying to solve. One way is personalizing the online shopping experience so that consumers only see the most relevant products to them.

5.2.5. Hyper-personalizing the Online Shopping Experience

Death by scrolling endless product display pages (PDP), which I'm sure many readers of this book that shop online have previously experienced. Sometimes, the online shopping experience can be filled with products being displayed that don't seem to match what you are looking for, whether that be a certain size, fit, silhouette, color, and so forth. This can cause a brand to lose customer retention, engagement, sales, and overall satisfaction with a brand's online experience. As explored in the previous section, this can lead to overconsumption as customers buy what they hope will be the right product fit for them, as most online retailers offer a free return policy, and thus, it is risk-free for the customer. One way to improve this dynamic and mitigate the need for returns for both retailer and customer is to enable e-commerce sites with personalization technology. In this context, online personalization means personalizing the online shopping and interactions that the customers make with the retailer's digital touchpoints across all types of devices.

Personalizing the shopping experience is one tool for instant fashion, with 71% of customers now expecting retailers to personalize the shopping journey just for them and 76% becoming frustrated when personalization doesn't happen (McKinsey 2021). There are many new innovations on the market that are tackling the personalization for fashion e-commerce from different angles such as Becoco with product display pages and True Fit from the size recommendation perspective (we'll talk more about sizing and fit in the next section). Regardless of the intentions of the tool, they all center around the utilization of artificial intelligence to analyze and understand the user's data to recommend the most relevant information on the screen. The data can be collected in various ways:

1. Web analytics tools

2. Urchin Tracking Module (UTM) Parameters on digital marketing campaigns

3. Questionnaires on a website or through an app

4. Customer relationship management systems

5. Point-of-sale (POS) systems

To provide instantaneous and seamless experiences, the data is often collected in real time as the customer is browsing. The outputs:

- Visual similarity: Which items are like the one that is currently being viewed.

- "Complete the look": Product recommendations to complete an outfit with the item that is currently being viewed.

- Curated product displays: Only relevant items are displayed on product display pages (and hopefully the end of death by scrolling). American online retailer Stitch Fix is one of the pioneers of curated fashion with the company reaching $2 billion in revenue in 2022 (Stitch Fix, 2022).

- Visual searches: The search box on a website has become a lot more powerful, and solutions are enabled with natural language processing. This means that phrases or non-product-specific keywords can be used to search for items.

- Styling advice: How to wear fashion can be as complicated as what to wear. AI stylists (often supported by human stylists) can propose styling advice, which can feel as if you were shopping offline in-store.

Since personalized online experiences are very tangible to see, with results of the deployed technologies easily measurable (click-through rates, sales increase, etc.), AI-powered personalization tools are indispensable for any online retailer. For example, sporting goods retailer

Decathlon partnered with search and discovery platform Algolia to enable search personalization. The results saw a 36% increase in click-through rate and a 50% increase in conversion rates (Algolia, 2023). These numbers are quite impressive. Retailers that are enabling hyper-personalization are seeing on average a 40% increase in revenue (McKinsey, 2021) with the benefits being retained customers, better produced engagement rates, and increased brand loyalty.

5.3. Online-Only Zone: Digital Assets

As we began to explore in Chapter 2, fashion design beyond physical products, fashion no longer means dealing with physical products that you can touch and feel but can also be purely digital. In Chapter 2, we explored it from the perspective of the designer being equipped with 3D digital design tools that enable the creation of digital products that can then be sold as NFTs, but what does digital fashion do for the general consumer? The boundaries between designer, retailer, buyer, and end user are blurring faster than ever in the online world. When it comes to creating, buying, and selling digital assets, the end consumer can do all these elements as more platforms become available. Research conducted by the digital fashion app OuttaWRLD showed that *"93% of digital fashion enthusiasts not only wanted to wear [and own] digital fashion but also wanted to create it too"* (Wilders, 2023). We'll explore the OuttaWRLD solution later in this chapter.

5.3.1. Buying Digital-Only Garments

Just like an online store for physical fashion garments, online stores for digital fashion started appearing around 2019 with the emergence of platforms such as RTFKT, DressX, The Dematerialised, and The Fabricant (Figures 5-5a, 5-5b, 5-5c). Each of these platforms allows customers to purchase digital-only assets (images, 3D files, moving content, etc.) in various ways including a variety of cryptocurrencies, digital/NFT wallets, and of course traditional money using bank cards. As discussed in Chapter 2, the assets are verified on the blockchain assigning the rightful owner to that asset. For the customer, it's like buying a car in the physical world and receiving legal paperwork from the local authorities proving that they are the legal owner and thus have full right to do whatever they want with the asset.

Regardless of the platform used to purchase the digital asset, the platforms mentioned have gained positive traction in the context of fashion because they have managed to create novel retail experiences for digital fashion. Going back to the notion that the lines are blurred between designer and customer, The Fabricant's agenda, for example, is *"from passive consumers we become active creators, monetizing our craft and sharing our creativity. Royalties are equally split among all participants involved in the co-creation of the digital fashion items"* (The Fabricant, 2023). This is reflected on their platform with the ability to co-create digital fashion. For RTFKT, owned by Nike, culture and community are extremely dominant in how their experience is delivered: *"RTFKT is a blueprint of a brand of the future: merging worlds via the combination of digital and physical craftsmanship, powered by a creative community, groundbreaking collaborations and non-stop innovation"* (RTFKT, 2023). To make it clearer, we broke it down.

Table 5-2. *Elements for driving digital assets*

Criteria	How	Experience
Scarcity	Exclusive drops, collabs, limited sales period	This drives the demand and value of the asset up. Customers pre-order or purchase immediately when an asset drops in the fear of missing out. RTFKT demonstrates this well with their sneaker drops and "forging" limited time events
Culture	Artists, brand partnerships, defined perspective, and voice	Customers and end users buy into a specific identity, which then is a reflection as to how the user is building their digital world. DressX demonstrates this with a multitude of brand partnerships including Adidas, Coca-Cola, and Warner Music
Community	Co-creation, social platforms, adjacent industries (sports, music, entertainment)	NFTs, crypto, and digital fashion are still in the early adoption phase, meaning communities are driving this category (as opposed to mass consumers). Discord is an important social platform for the digital fashion communities to gather to discuss, share, and drive product development
Hype	Influencers, celebrity, NFT market fluctuations	In 2021, RTFKT generated $3.1M worth of digital sneakers in seven minutes (RTFKT, 2021). The power of a well-known crypto-artist and the boom of NFTs amalgamated in hype and rapid sales. Momentum is key in the fast-moving digital space

Figure 5-5a. *The Fabricant Studio, Season 0 Collection*

Figure 5-5b. *The Fabricant and Zeeuws Museum Collaboration Collection entitled "WHOLE"*

Figure 5-5c. *The Fabricant, Night Time*

Although we love the way that digital fashion is heading, we must look at the flip side too. NFTs and digital assets are nascent, meaning that the value of assets goes up and down according to the state of the crypto market. However, according to Morgan Stanley, the luxury NFT market could reach $56 billion by 2030 (Lee, 2021). Therefore, retail platforms that facilitate such retailing between NFT creators and the buyer, and trading between NFT owners are required, which will become more sophisticated over time. We suggest that any reader of this book conduct their own research if they are intending to purchase a digital fashion asset.

5.3.2. Shoppable Virtual Worlds

We've discussed a lot about fashion products that only exist in the digital form, but how about retail destinations that only exist as virtual experiences? As we've seen from companies like AnamXR and Fashion Innovation Agency earlier in the book, the technology is now available to create virtual worlds in high fidelity for marketing purposes. For fashion brands, virtual worlds that are also retail outlets offer an extra layer of brand engagement and retail experience either through a regular desktop computer, a mobile device, or in virtual reality through goggles such as Oculus Quest. Products on display are either digital twins or are photographs rendered to be suitable for the virtual environment. For the customer, it's as if you're in the physical store with the ability to get up close to the product, read product information, and of course purchase. So far, many brands are creating virtual retail stores as stand-alone one-off or seasonal experiences as the investment into such projects is still relatively high. Combined with the need for maintenance if the store is a longer-term project makes it an expensive endeavor. Hence, shoppable virtual worlds are still only accessible to the larger brands.

Companies such as Emperia and Obsess are two examples of companies that are building virtual stores on behalf of fashion brands. Obsess works with brands such as Ralph Lauren and Lee, in which they have replicated physical stores to deliver what they call *"experiential e-commerce."* What this means is that e-commerce is being delivered away from the traditional grid format where the user scrolls through hundreds of products on the product discovery page. This results in an experience where you browse as if you were in-store physically. Both Emperia and Obsess are creating complete shoppable virtual worlds, taking online shopping to the next level to create differentiation for the customer. As Olga Dogadkina (2023), co-founder and CEO of Emperia, tells us:

> *"From a brand perspective, everything they do in-store, every bit of differentiation that they would put in, for example Dior wouldn't look the same as Louis Vuitton, it helps the customer to tell the brands apart. However, online if you remove the fonts and the logo, the shopping experience is exactly the same on each website and it's very difficult for the customer to navigate or differentiate within the online environment."*

Figure 5-6a. *Emperia's campaign for Harrods and Dior Beauty*

Dogadkina's strive to help brands differentiate their experiences online led to her first project with London's luxury department store Harrods (Figure 5-6a), which allowed Emperia to create a blueprint for shoppable virtual worlds that other brands can easily deploy. To make it happen technically, Emperia's platform connects to the brand's stock management system (software such as Sortly or ApparelMagic) to ensure seamless real-time stock and price updates in the virtual world. This ease of integration is also translated by connecting to the brand's own online checkout system whereby any product added to the cart in the virtual world is already there on the store's usual checkout system. This seamlessness is what's going to get us shopping (like in the Ralph Lauren store in Figure 5-6c)! Brands wishing to work with Emperia go through a two-step integration process:

1. Technical, as just explained.

2. Virtual store buildout, taking on average between six and eight weeks.

It doesn't stop just at online stores. Emperia worked with Tommy Hilfiger for their activation during Metaverse Fashion Week 2023 (Figure 5-6b) that allowed visitors to purchase physical and digital Tommy Hilfiger products. Interoperability was the keyword for the Tommy Hilfiger activation whereby the project blended several platforms together including Decentraland, Roblox, Spatial, DressX, and Ready Player Me. The aggregation of several platforms into one experience demonstrates just how sophisticated the virtual shopping space is getting and undoubtedly will become more accessible across platforms as the space speeds up. Combined with Emperia's data suite to see which parts of the virtual store are performing with elements such as 3D environment heatmapping, brands have a new powerful way to engage with their shoppers virtually. *"Compared to regular brand websites, we generally see an average of 11 minutes engagement time, 73% uplift on conversion rates and about 750% ROI. Our best performing experience to date was Dior's Christmas grocery store and beauty, which saw an average engagement time of 18 minutes"* (Dogadkina, 2023).

Figure 5-6b. *Emperia's campaign for Tommy Hilfiger during Metaverse Fashion Week 2023*

Figure 5-6c. *Emperia's campaign for Ralph Lauren*

Figure 5-6d. *Emperia's campaign for Lacoste*

Figure 5-6e. *Example of products inside Lacoste's virtual world created by Emperia*

From a business strategy perspective, virtual stores allow for stronger brand positioning, engagement, and tapping into different demographics such as Emperia's project with Lacoste (Figures 5-6d and 5-6e) focusing on driving Gen Z engagement. Virtual stores are the next level of omnichannel retailing that brands can tap into as an extension to their retail channels. Omnichannel is described as *"seamless and effortless, high-quality customer experiences that occur within and between contact channels"* (Butte, 2015). Although omnichannel is not a new concept since the dawn of e-commerce, what this chapter highlights is that there's no longer the separation of physical retail or digital retail, but just retail that caters to the ever-changing way that consumers want to experience fashion. It's now the fashion retailer's job to place whatever experience that works for their customer base's attention span.

5.3.3. Overlaying Digital onto the Physical: Creating and Buying in an AR Retail Experience

From digital fashion stores (DressX, etc.), to shopping games (like the ones that AnamXR has created) and shoppable virtual worlds (Emperia), and now to creating and buying digital assets in augmented reality. As we've explored previously, the ability to wear or try on clothing digitally through AR on a mobile device is creating a fun experience with digital fashion; however, to design digital fashion products in AR and then purchase the finished asset is still emerging. OuttaWRLD, an app that allows users to create and customize digital garments in real-time augmented reality, is pushing the boundaries as to how virtual fashion interacts with the physical world. The platform was born out of the founder's, Charles Wilders, frustration of not being able to be more creative with digital fashion as a buyer and end user: *"our mission is to empower everybody to create and purchase their own digital fashion. The buyer wants to be able to manipulate products and OuttaWRLD facilitates this through personalization and customization in AR. We confirmed this through our user testing (referring to the 93% of users at the start of this section) that when people are engaging with digital fashion, it must reflect them and their personality"* (Wilders, 2023).

Wilders explains to make AR digital fashion happen, the digital assets and foundations of the design tool must be put through the process of being rigged onto the virtual body via an exoskeleton. At the time of writing this book, it takes one week to rig ten digital garments, meaning that the process is slow. However, this is what gives the OuttaWRLD user the ability to design on a human body through AR and is a vital component to the solution. Paired with low latency (delay), the platform gives the illusion that the digital garment is being worn on the physical body. Think of the Wanna virtual try-on earlier in this chapter. The extension of identity and the physical body (Figures 5-7a and 5-7d) being visible with the AR garment is what Wilders aims to excite the customer: *"one user said to us 'this looks like it gives you superpowers.' That's the feeling that we want to create with our digital fashion"* (2023.)

Aside from the creation feature of OuttaWRLD (as shown in Figures 5-7b and 5-7c), the retail side in AR is an important element to finish the customer experience and how brands can capitalize on the increase of AR utilization. Worldwide there are expected to be 1.7 billion user devices by 2024 (Statista, 2022), and retailers that are capitalizing on AR technology are seeing up to 40% higher conversion rates when utilized as part of an advertising campaign (Joshi, 2023). Wilders expects that the retailing of digital fashion assets will become a virtuous circle for all involved to benefit from. *"The outtaWRLD token will be the currency in the app. If someone's created an asset with a digital texture (Figures 5-7b and 5-7c) that's being used in a very popular digital garment, the owner of that digital texture will collect remuneration"* (Wilders, 2023).

In the future for customers, creating, selling, and buying in AR will be as normal as shopping on a standard e-commerce store. More plug-and-play AR retail solutions will also eventually appear on the market that will enable brands to tap into AR retail with ease, just like Shopify. However, Wilders does lament that for true interoperability to happen within the metaverse and virtual worlds, brands need to get more comfortable of not having complete control or ownership as to how their brand worlds and digital products will be crafted since co-creation is happening with the customers. At present, from research, Wilders does not feel that brands being comfortable is happening fast enough.

Escapism, ultimately what digital fashion allows, is how brands should approach layering such technology into their retail channels. Success metrics for platforms such as OuttaWRLD, or any featured in this book, not only include traditional metrics such as app downloads, social shares, or volume of trading but should also consider the fact that customers are creators of their assets. This means that when wearing digital fashion in AR for social sharing is as normal as wearing physical clothes, this will be a major success indicator that technologies can work. *"It's always difficult to do the switch when it's not part of your [retail] DNA, and so brands must make sure that there is an authentic strategy to go into this digital space"* (Romero, 2022). The OuttaWRLD app launch focus is a B2C retail offering, but the goal is to eventually allow other retailers and brands to capitalize on the technology. Perhaps another brand could topple Nike from the top of the fashion NFT leaderboard?

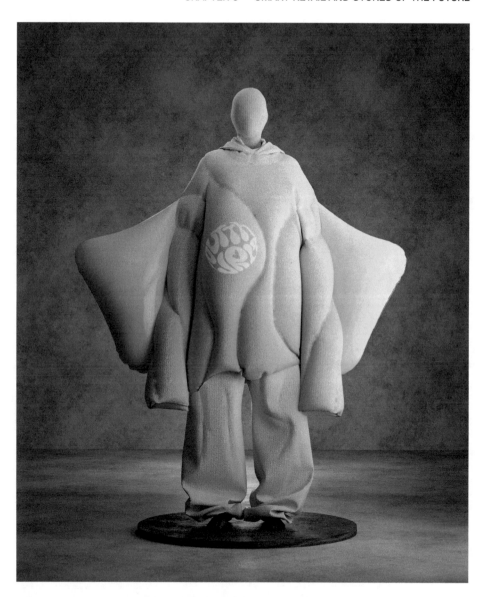

Figure 5-7a. *OuttaWRLD's first digital fashion customizable collection*

Figure 5-7b. *OuttaWRLD app customizing skin textures*

Figure 5-7c. *OuttaWRLD app customizing animated meshes*

Figure 5-7d. *OuttaWRLD customized digital garment end result overlaid in AR*

One retail use case that has passed the retail proof of concept is the marketplace for digital fashion, such as DressX. The quality of digital fashion, in terms of design and resolution, has become high enough for customers to want to pay money to utilize them in a manner for content such as social media. Figure 5-8 is an example of Peter dressed in a digital garment purchased from DressX, which the brand Porka_X's digital garment was superimposed onto a ready-made image. In this instance, there is no ownership of the garment, but a purchaser-owned final image to be used wherever they wish to do so. However, many digital fashion enthusiasts now also want to legally own their digital fashion purchases as NFTs, which has been a recurring theme throughout this book. It makes it ideal for digital assets such as digital fashion as it cannot be copied, substituted, or subdivided, meaning that the true owner can always be verified. Moving into the next 10 to 15 years, this will enable brands small and big to think about their retail business models in a different way.

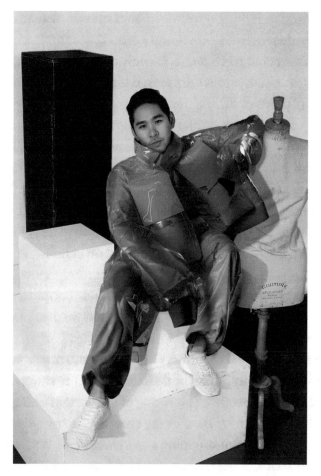

Figure 5-8. *Peter dressed in a digital garment purchased from DressX*

5.4. Building a Tech-Enabled Retail Platform

With all that we have discussed in the book until now, we have focused on the application of externally developed technologies to fashion brands and discovering the potential transformation from this synergy. The other side of the coin lies within the companies that aim to develop both the technologies and fashion, innovating in both spaces. Instead of partnering with the opposite (e.g., a fashion brand partnering with a tech company to benefit from the technical elements for only the fitting part of the shopping experience), these companies are focused on innovating different parts of their own retail processes throughout the customer shopping experience with the help of technology. While we define this as a "tech-enabled" retail platform, others have named this "augmented retail" (Gokal, 2019).

Take Amazon for instance; while they may sell all categories from home furniture to stationery, when taking a deeper look into their fashion category, one can see the efforts toward innovation. One of the most interesting is the Amazon Prime Try Before You Buy. The ability to order products online, receive them to physically try on at home, and then return any of the items without making any financial commitments. This is in response to the customer who prefers on-demand shopping, as well as linking back to the "work from home" culture that we previously spoke about in Section 4.1.1.

This type of offering to customers becomes more of a service of convenience that directly allows more freedom for the shopper from a business model perspective. This is one of the current examples of a service that is created and hosted by the company themselves without an intermediary during the shopping experience itself. While this is more on the lo-fi side of tech (where the tech is not revolutionary but rather less complex and based on the e-commerce platform), it remains relevant to what we have seen so far about the current mindset of the industry in terms of keeping most things traditional while adding just a small bit of innovation where desired by the company. The same can be said for the B2C showrooming that works in this omnichannel concept where the online selections are also made available in the physical store for purchasing without the full usual physical shopping described in Section 5.1.

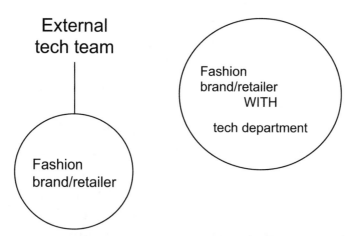

Figure 5-9. *Diagram of externally sourced tech solution collaborations with brands/retailers vs. brands/retailers with a tech department*

On the other hand, Amazon has also tapped into hard tech as they have taken their e-commerce to a physical version, meaning that the shopping experience mirrors the typical physical shopping journey but with more advanced technologies embedded into it such as touchscreens in fitting rooms to rate the selected products. It "is described as a mix of Amazon Style app-based interactions, in-store styling-and-fitting services, online-to-IRL try-ons, and Amazon One palm-recognition-based checkouts—a blend of data-driven technology that makes the customer journey unique in the fashion space" (Lo, 2022). This is different to the collaborations discussed in Section 5.1, since the technologies here are part of the full shopping experience from start to finish as opposed to a tech partner being added to one part of the journey. Figure 5-9 illustrates this where the structure on the left displays an external tech team offering their solution to the fashion brand or retailer vs. the structure on the right that represents a tech department being part of the brand or retailer itself as a more permanent department.

We saw earlier that a collaborating tech company may be added to only the payment or the changing room parts of the shopping experience. This time, with Amazon Style's physical retail store in the United States, technologies transform the full experience, making it heavily dependent on the QR codes attached to the fashion items. These QR codes allow communication between the shopper, the app, and the shop floor to allow more streamlined shopping experiences such as automatically placing the scanned items into the fitting rooms ready to try on. This is completed by the desired items readily placed at the till for pickup and payment. The usual process of picking up products from shelves and rails is changed to a more digital-based user journey that requires the smartphone throughout the experience along with the interactive screens, hence why we refer to this as a "tech-enabled" platform.

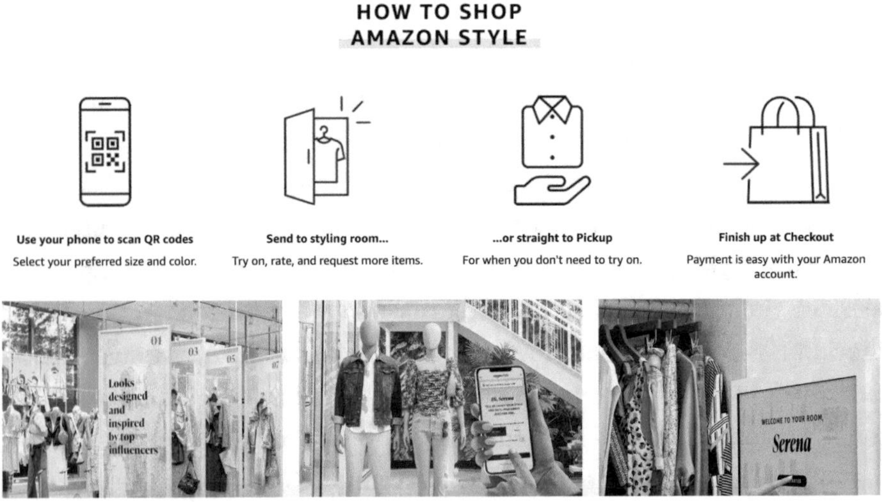
HOW TO SHOP
AMAZON STYLE
Use your phone to scan QR codes
Select your preferred size and color.
Send to styling room...
Try on, rate, and request more items.
...or straight to Pickup
For when you don't need to try on.
Finish up at Checkout
Payment is easy with your Amazon account.
Looks designed and inspired by top influencers
WELCOME TO YOUR ROOM,
Serena

Figure 5-10. *Amazon Style user journey*

The purpose of applying multiple technologies in one space is a special case for companies like Amazon given their dedication to multiple industries as opposed to fashion alone unlike fashion brands. The purpose of this tech-focused physical shopping experience "is to make shopping more inspiring, personalized, and convenient for each customer" according to the managing director of Amazon Style (2022). This is what would be described as an example of acquiring or collaborating with other tech elements to build on top of the existing shopping format to push these purposes. Co-CEO of Marks & Spencer Katie Bickerstaffe highlighted this when speaking about their strategy. Even though the context was more to do with implementing AI particularly on the M&S.com website, the same notion is applicable to all other elements of the physical shopping experiences:

> *"...a 'buy not build' approach – enabling us to accelerate our personalization strategy by integrating the market leading tech on M&S.com in under 12 months. We're taking personalization to the next level to inspire our customers with tailored outfit inspiration... We already know the incremental value personalization can bring and we anticipate that personalization will generate more than £100m of annualized incremental revenue for the business." (Katie Bickerstaffe, 2022)*

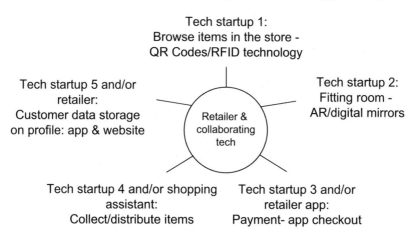

Figure 5-11. *Diagram of tech startups feeding different solutions into brands/retailers' tech-enabled physical store like Store of the Future by Farfetch*

The retailer Farfetch has focused on this type of activity as they have previously created a physical store that was also "tech enabled" in 2017 after two years of development. Similarly to the Amazon Style store, the Farfetch "Store of the Future" consisted of a shopping journey that embedded tech throughout while fully connected to the customer's smartphone. From the moment a customer entered the store, the connection between their smartphone and store elements through RFID meant that the shopping journeys could be tracked per customer to allow the personalized experience throughout, even when they have completely left the store and viewing their wish list, which will be described further in this section. Different tech companies have developed these elements externally to allow Farfetch to integrate into their app to make this whole experience possible (illustrated in Figure 5-11). According to the founder and CEO at Farfetch, José Neves, they have been "working with RFID companies, [and] with hologram companies [as] it's not like [they're] going to build all this stuff [themselves]" (2017). Various parts of the shopping journey would all connect to the retailer's main system where all data would be stored including the shopping habits of the customers. These elements developed included

> *"...a universal login that recognises a customer as she checks into the store; an RFID-enabled clothing rack that detects which products she is browsing and auto-populates her wishlist; a digital mirror that allows her to view her wishlist and summon items in different sizes and colors; a mobile payment experience similar to what exists in Apple Stores; and, of course, the underlying data layer that connects these services with each other and the Farfetch platform." (Neves, 2017)*

As this was a beta test, there was plenty of room for development that remains publicly unexplored as the store has discontinued in the meantime. While the future developments could introduce other technologically advanced attributes, what is evident in the meantime from this particular trial is that:

1. This shopping journey saw more data collected of customers compared to the newer Amazon Style store – for example, a simple picking up and looking at a product would add it to the customer's wish list, even if the customer's intentions were not for this compared to needing to scan the QR codes for a clearer indication as with Amazon Style (Porter, 2022).

2. All of this data would not be possible to obtain without the involvement of the customer downloading the Farfetch app. This is a step that would require additional efforts by the customer before entering the store as opposed to the conventional shopping experience. This means a potential no-commitment system could encourage even more customers to participate in the full shopping experience.

3. The technology is predominantly more simplified from the Amazon Style store as touchscreens have been installed as opposed to the digital mirrors in the Store of the Future. This is an indicator of the development of interactive screens or at least the decisions of which technologies to adopt in a more recent period compared to 2017.

These are both omnichannel retailers; however, one is in fashion (Farfetch), while the other is known as a technology company (Amazon). What's interesting to point out is that Farfetch has moved on from this to provide all of the aforementioned in one of their acquired brand stores in London, Browns. This becomes a different use case where the host of the store is the acquired brand as opposed to the retailer.

5.5. Chapter Summary

When analyzing these efforts, it's interesting to note that we end where it all started: brick and mortar. As much as we can speak about how AI is revolutionizing the Internet, or how much AR is helping businesses run remotely, one thing that seems to never completely disappear is the implementation of technologies in physical stores. Forecast reports have shown that the industry will not run away from the physical shopping experiences anytime soon with figures showing that offline sales are estimated to be worth $309 billion, specifically within the luxury market, let alone the overall fashion retail market at different market levels (McKinsey & Company, 2018).

What we can learn from this chapter:

1. There is a balance between innovation being done online and physical shopping experiences.

2. There is a growing interest in purchasing digital-only garments, meaning more demand for NFTs by fashion brands across different platforms that don't directly link with fashion, for example, gaming platforms.

3. Retail can also invite the user to interact beyond trying on a garment but also to personalize it.

Activity: **Physical store safari**

Find a physical store near you to explore the technologies in person.

Table 5-3. *Table of physical in-store experiences*

Technology, company	Store, location
Body scanning	
FIT:MATCH.ai	Macy's, United States
	Savage X Fenty, Lenox Square Mall location in Atlanta, Georgia
Treedy's	Decathlon, Rennes, France
Augmented shopping experience	
Augmented retail experience: Amazon Style store	The Americana at Brand in Glendale, California, and the other at Easton Town Center in Columbus, Ohio, USA
Augmented retail experience: Browns (white label solution by Farfetch)	Browns Flagship boutique, Brook Street, UK
Automated self-checkout: MishiPay	Flying Tiger, Copenhagen and UK

CHAPTER 6

Minimum Effort, Maximum Output

6.1. The Winners Are Tech Savvy

Budgets for innovation, either for technology or other forms of innovation, are often quite low for fashion brands compared to other budget lines such as marketing or distribution. According to McKinsey & Co (2022), "in 2021 fashion companies invested between 1.6 and 1.8 percent of their revenues in technology. By 2030, that figure is expected to rise to between 3.0 and 3.5 percent." Even by the time 2030 rolls around, innovation budgets will still be small. This means that for many fashion brands, the expectations will be that fashion tech deployments should garner maximum output or return for very minimal effort or investment. This is slightly paradoxical as technology does require more initial outlay before the rewards can be reaped.

As we have seen throughout the various case studies in this book, the winners are the brands that are placing tech at the core of their businesses. Whether that be Anne-Christine's intrapreneurial solution of digital lookbooks to unite and streamline sales and marketing across Tommy Hilfiger globally, or Nike's strategic acquisition of an external startup to place them at the top of the charts as the brand that is generating the most revenue from digital assets. We believe that companies that don't want to end up in bankruptcy like some of their peers in recent years should make tech a strategic part of their business; thus facilitating differentiation.

Tech is helping fashion brands and retailers to win, and this is shown by the interest in technology companies being acquired by retailers. For example, Farfetch has acquired several tech companies including Wanna, as explored in Chapter 5; Luxclusif, a resale tech company; and Allure Systems, an AI-powered image creation platform. These acquisitions are an indicator that technologies are fundamental in shaping how fashion brands will be creating value moving forward and what retailers should be thinking about to stay ahead. Although it may not always be rosy in a fashion tech startup's trajectory, such as AI-powered styling platform and retailer Thread.com's bankruptcy in late 2022, the technology and IP itself were acquired by UK retailer Marks & Spencer in early 2023. Regardless of if a company deploys a build or buy approach when it comes to integrating tech, the point is that fashion retailers should be proactively upgrading their business models and operations to stay a winner.

6.2. Irrelevancy Is Real

For the losers (or struggling retailers), the possibility of becoming irrelevant in the fashion landscape is very real. As discussed in Chapters 4 and 5, consumer attitudes and behavior are changing, and expectations from the brands that they love are ever evolving. Whether it be adopting more sustainable practices and integrating tech such as white labeled resale, rental, or repair platforms, or tapping into social commerce and shoppable media content, each of these small activations contributes to a brand's overall cultural and societal relevance.

The technology itself must also stay relevant. AI is a good example of where bias needs to be mitigated to ensure that brands do not use insights, creations, or the recommendations outputted that could alienate certain market segments. As discussed in Chapter 4, tech has still yet to come a long way with being truly inclusive. This can be challenging as many data sets that brands have are not necessarily all encompassing when it comes to demographics and geographical locations. Therefore, platforms could fall into the trap of delivering solutions to only able-bodied, Caucasian body features and slim fit. Brands such as denim brand, Levi's, are taking steps to ensure that they are diverse and inclusive as much as possible by partnering with Lalaland, an AI-powered digital model creation software, to display a wider diverse range of models. The fashion brand notes:

"When we say supplement, we mean the AI-generated models can be used in conjunction with human models to potentially expand the number of models per product. We are excited about a world where consumers can see more models on our site, potentially reflecting any combination of body type, age, size, race, and ethnicity, enabling us to create a more personal and inclusive shopping experience." (Demopoulos, 2023)

Technology of course can only facilitate relevancy and not fabricate it. Forever 21, Victoria's Secret, and Abercrombie & Fitch are some example brands that have struggled to stay relevant in recent years, which have faced administration or revenue declines. Perhaps they could utilize tech in a savvier way to help them?

6.3. Upskilling the Future Workforce

The users of the technologies explored are not just the customers making the purchases of the products but also those working in the fashion brands behind the scenes in the headquarters as explored in Chapter 1. If they aren't trained properly, then there is a chance that the brand does not keep up to date with what is required to stay relevant in the industry.

For example, without 3D digital designers within their departments (if they aren't outsourced), then the brand will not be able to produce digital assets explored in Chapters 2 and 3. Upskilling can make all the difference for the individual employees who can stay relevant even for future roles, while the brands can benefit from these skills in the long run.

It is understandable that this can be a costly process from the training itself. For instance, "Amazon, as part of its "Upskilling 2025" initiative, is investing $1.2 billion to train more than 300,000 employees for higher-skilled jobs as automation eliminates many existing roles" (BOF, 2023). The funds required to purchase the hardware or software can also increase these costs, which can deter fashion brands from investing further into this; however, return on investment can make this worthwhile. According to the McKinsey report, "education and training typically generate [a] return on investment that is between two-and-a-half and three times higher than recruiting" even during "economically uncertain times" (McKinsey, 2022).

This, paired with hiring more C-suite roles that focus on specialities such as sustainability, marketing, digital innovation, and diversity and inclusion, can further flip the traditional departments in the headquarters where all decisions are made for the rest of the supply chain (McKinsey, 2022). As the Gen Z and Generation Alpha enter into the industry, particularly those similar to the ones discussed in Chapter 1 who are already introduced to these technologies during their education, will also have an impact on the skill set they will already bring to the industry before any further training by the fashion brands they get employed by.

6.4. What Happens Next?

This book has shown us that there are opportunities across the entire fashion value chain for technology to transform each part. The potential for innovation and disruption is high, with areas such as retail being well underway and others like design and creative relatively still ripe for further transformation. It would be futile for us to "predict the future" of fashion tech and the impact it will have in general on the industry. However, fashion tech is going to be a huge category; there are approximately 35,000 companies identified as fashion in the tech space, and they have fundraised from investors approximately $45 billion by June 2023 (Tracxn, 2023). Rather than highlighting any one technology, it'd be more pertinent to highlight where it will take us. Some areas that excite us are as follows:

> Legacy systems transitioning into automated processes and infrastructure: This is where AI can truly shape the way the business of fashion is going to function and how fashion professionals perform their jobs. Think generative design, smoother production system, improved supply chain and logistics, and smart retailing.

> Knowledge and ownership at the employees' and customers' fingertips: The industry is no longer able to hide. Where products come from, what their materials contain, and how they're made are just as important as the brand experience. New ownership models are key for creators and resale models. Think transparency, digital passports and identities, and traceable suppliers.

> Physical fashion augmented by extreme digitalization, the metaverse, and content: In a world where most fashion products are generic, brands will need to extend their brand experiences beyond the physical product. Think digital assets, virtual worlds, and the merger of online and offline retail.

> From linear to circular: The hardest shift of all, since
> fashion has been linear ever since the industrial
> revolution; however, technologies to combat
> overconsumption and overproduction will be key
> to sustainable growth. Think end-of-life and
> re-commerce tech, regenerative materials, and a
> new layer of services to facilitate circularity.

Eventually many of the technologies mentioned in this book will become tools in the background for the everyday running and consumption of fashion, just like a smartphone or the Internet. Fashion tech has the capacity to significantly reconfigure the business of fashion, and CEOs need to place it high on the agenda to tackle some of the industry's toughest challenges. For an industry estimated to be $3 trillion very soon, which touches every part of the world and nearly every human being's life, fundamental shifts will need to be had to keep it churning.

6.4.1. Summary of Must-Have vs. Nice-to-Have Technologies in Fashion Brands

If industry failures (as well as successes) have taught us anything, it is that there are some "must-haves" as well as "nice-to-haves" (Table 6-1) when considering technology in fashion. Not every solution will benefit every brand in the same way for varying reasons that this book has revealed; however, some can drastically change the business models, design and manufacturing processes, and how overall the brands connect with their customers.

Table 6-1. *Table of must-have vs nice-to-have tech solutions*

Must-have tech solutions:	Nice-to-have tech solutions:
Help the industry with important matters such as sustainability, time efficiency, and cost efficiency according to what has been explored in this book	Good ideas that are not trivial to transforming the industry
Production	
AI pattern cutting software (lay planning, digitizing, etc.)	Traceability tech (linking to blockchain for certification)
Repair system (including lo-fi tech e-commerce platform)	
Design	
	No-skill generative design software
	3D digital design software
Marketing	
AR virtual try-on	VR virtual worlds (including B2B showrooms, Web3 stores)
Retail	
Body scanning (including AI size recommendations and avatar creation)	Automated fitting room (including AR interactive screens/mirrors)
Automated payment systems (including RFID)	ID passports with QR codes
	Fully augmented tech-enabled physical store

Glossary

Word/phrase	Definition	Pages
Additive manufacturing	The general industrial term to describe the production of a 3D object one layer at a time, for example, 3D printing	
Anti-waste law for a circular economy (AGEC)	A French law passed in 2020 that aims to fight against waste and encourages businesses to shift toward a circular economy in France	
Algorithm	A set of instructions used in calculations to solve problems, usually in computer science	
Artificial intelligence	A branch of computer science referring to the intelligence of software or machines mimicking that of humans	
Augmented product	A product that has been enhanced beyond its core purpose with services and features to provide the customer with extra benefits, for example, Aftercare	
Augmented reality	An interactive experience where a computer-generated image is superimposed onto the user's view of the real world	
Brand(s)	A product, service, or concept that is delivered by a specific company under a particular name. In fashion, this is quite often under the founding designer's name, for example, Gucci or Prada	

(continued)

Word/phrase	Definition	Pages
Fashion buyer	A job role that involves an individual selecting and purchasing which products to be sold through their retail channels	
Consumer	The term to describe a person or group of people that purchases products or services, primarily for their personal use	
Circular economy	An economic system and model whereby products are reused and regenerated to keep materials in circulation for longer prior to becoming waste	
Digital fashion	Fashion products that only exist in the digital form and are visually represented and created using 3D software such as CLO3D or Browzwear	
Dwell time	The length of time a user or a customer spends in one place looking at a specific element of a brand, for example, a product in a retail store or a product description page online	
Back-end technologies	Technologies that are the foundations of how a program operates, but not the final product, for example, AR for virtual try-on apps	
Direct to consumer (D2C)	A business model where products are sold by the brand directly to the consumer without the need of a third party. For example, Warby Parker sells eyewear to consumers without the intervention of an optician	
Digital showroom	Also referred to as a virtual showroom, is an online platform that enables brands to showcase and sell products digitally	

(continued)

Word/phrase	Definition	Pages
Distributor	An agent that represents brands to supply their goods to their distribution channels, such as an independent retailer	
Experiential e-commerce	A marketing strategy that utilizes experiential technologies such as AR and VR to immerse the customer in the brand's world, thus strengthening the brand to customer connection	
Fashion designer	A job role involving an individual designing and developing fashion collections	
Front-end technologies	Software and hardware that the user interacts with directly, for example, website	
Gimmicky tech	Technologies that have a novelty aspect, usually for short-term gains and/or marketing purposes without a deep business purpose, for example, Google Glass	
Hard tech	Physical technologies such as devices or machinery that may consist of many components, for example, sewing machine	
Non-fungible token (NFT)	Blockchain-based tokens that each represent a unique asset like a piece of art, digital content, or media	
Internet of Things (IoT)	The interconnection via the Internet of computing devices embedded in everyday objects, enabling them to send and receive data	
Last mile	Short geographical segment of delivery of communication and media services or the delivery of products to customers located in dense areas	

(continued)

Word/phrase	Definition	Pages
Made-to-order	Specially made according to a customer's specifications	
Marketeers	A person who sells goods or services in a market	
Minimum viable product (MVP)	A version of a product gathering only the elementary functionalities when it is launched on the market	
Mixed reality	An emergent technology that blends virtual reality (VR) and augmented reality (AR)	
Product display pages (PDP)	Web page that outlines everything customers and buyers need to know about a particular product – including information about color, sizing, material, pricing, shipping options, and more	
Pop-up store	Shop or store that is deliberately temporary	
Preloved	An item that is secondhand	
Profit and loss (P&L)	Financial statement that summarizes the revenues, costs, and expenses incurred during a specified period, usually a quarter or fiscal year	
Production	Action of making or manufacturing from components or raw materials, or the process of being so manufactured	
Product lifecycle management (PLM) systems	Handling of a good as it moves through the typical stages of its product life: development and introduction, growth, maturity/stability, and decline	
Proof-of-attendance protocol (POAP)	Non-fungible tokens (NFTs) that prove a person has attended a certain event	

(continued)

Word/phrase	Definition	Pages
Recommerce	Selling of previously owned items through online marketplaces to buyers who reuse, recycle, or resell them	
Retail	Sale of goods to the public in relatively small quantities for use or consumption rather than for resale	
Retailer	Person or business that sells goods to the public in relatively small quantities for use or consumption rather than for resale	
RFID	Technology that uses radio waves to passively identify a tagged object	
Return on investment (ROI)	Performance measure used to evaluate the efficiency or profitability of an investment or compare the efficiency of a number of different investments	
Slow fashion	Describes clothing designs seen on the catwalk and rapidly become trends implemented in stores in bulk units	
Soft tech	Technologies that include the human areas of decision-making, strategy development, training, and concept formation	
Startup	Company in the first stages of operations	
Supply chain	Network of individuals and companies who are involved in creating a product and delivering it to the consumer	
Sustainability	Ability to maintain or support a process continuously over time	

(*continued*)

Word/phrase	Definition	Pages
Sustainable	Something able to be maintained at a certain rate or level. In this context, relating to longevity of materials	
Value chain	Process in which businesses receive raw materials, add value to them through production, manufacturing, and other processes to create a finished product, and then sell the finished product to consumers	
Virtual worlds/shop	Computer-simulated representation of the "real world" with specific spatial and physical characteristics where users can interact virtually	

Bibliography

3DLOOK – AI-powered 3D Body Measuring Solution. [online]
3DLOOK. Available at https://3dlook.ai/ (Accessed March 10, 2023).

Absolutely Courier (2022). Fashion and Retail – the Evolving Last-Mile Delivery Challenge. Available at www.absolutelycourier.com/fashion-and-retail-the-evolving-last-mile-delivery-challenge/ (Accessed October 12, 2023).

Actian (2023). 5 Tips to Transition from Multichannel to Omnichannel. Available at www.actian.com/blog/data-integration/multichannel-to-omnichannel/#:~:text=According%20to%20Frost%20%26%20Sullivan%2C%20omnichannel,stage%20of%20the%20buyer's%20journey (Accessed June 14, 2023).

Albella, E., Balchandani, A., Cornbleet, N., and Lee, L. (2022). Retail Practice. [online] Available at www.mckinsey.com/~/media/mckinsey/industries/retail/our%20insights/in%20search%20of%20fashions%20sustainability%20seekers/in-search-of-fashions-sustainability-seekers.pdf (Accessed March 16, 2023).

Albrighi, L. (2023). Metaverse and Mixing Digital with Physical Marketing. Interviewed by Von N. Ruzive (Zoom), May 8.

Algolia (2023). Decathlon Singapore: Driving 50% Higher Conversion Rate with Omnichannel, Personalized Search. Available at https://resources.algolia.com/customer-stories/casestudy-decathlon-singapore (Accessed October 13, 2023).

Alsop, T. (2022). Number of mobile augmented reality (AR) active user devices worldwide from 2019 to 2024. Available at www.statista.com/statistics/1098630/global-mobile-augmented-reality-ar-users/ (Accessed October 13, 2023).

BIBLIOGRAPHY

Amazon (n.d.). Amazon Style. [online] Amazon.com. Available at www.amazon.com/b?ie=UTF8&node=23676409011 (Accessed June 7, 2023).

Amazon (n.d.). Amazon.com Help: Prime Try Before You Buy. [online] www.amazon.com. Available at www.amazon.com/gp/help/customer/display.html?nodeId=GCQDLMG7C2YEXSM4 (Accessed June 7, 2023).

Andreani, J.B. (2023). Fashion Tech in Education at IFA Paris. Interviewed by Von N. Ruzive (Zoom). March 9.

Andreessen, M. (2011). Software Is Eating the World. Available at https://a16z.com/2011/08/20/why-software-is-eating-the-world/ (Accessed June 23, 2022).

Aquino, S. (2022). Facebook Parent Company Meta Introduces More Inclusive Avatars for Disabled People, Super Bowl LVI. [online] Forbes. Available at www.forbes.com/sites/stevenaquino/2022/02/01/facebook-parent-company-meta-introduces-more-inclusive-avatars-for-disabled-people-super-bowl-lvi/ [Accessed Aug. 12, 2022].

Arkhangelskiy, S. (2023). Virtual Try-On with WANNA. Interviewed by Von N. Ruzive (Zoom). May 18, 2023.

Arora, N., Ensslen, D., Fiedler, L., Liu, W.W., Robinson, K., Stein, E., and Schüler, G. (2021). The value of getting personalization right—or wrong—is multiplying. Available at www.mckinsey.com/capabilities/growth-marketing-and-sales/our-insights/the-value-of-getting-personalization-right-or-wrong-is-multiplying (Accessed May 31, 2023).

Arthur, R. (2016). Stella McCartney On Innovating The Fashion Industry From Within. [online] Forbes. Available at www.forbes.com/sites/rachelarthur/2016/11/20/stella-mccartney-innovation-sustainability/ [Accessed June 12, 2023].

Bain, M. (2023). Generative AI Is Proving a Tough Sell to Fashion's Next Generation. Available at www.businessoffashion.com/articles/technology/generative-ai-is-proving-a-tough-sell-to-fashions-next-generation/ (Accessed June 12, 2023).

Balenciaga (n.d.). Balenciaga | Fall 21. [online] videogame.balenciaga. com. Available at `https://videogame.balenciaga.com/en/` [Accessed July 2, 2023].

Benedetto, S. (2023). Queen of Raw: MateriaMX. Interviewed by Peter Jeun Ho Tsang (Google Meet), June 27, 2023.

Blanco, R. (2023). Digital Vs Physical B2B Showrooms. Interviewed by Von N. Ruzive (Zoom). January 5.

Bof Team and McKinsey & Company (2023). The State of Fashion 2023. [online] Available at `www.mckinsey.com/~/media/mckinsey/industries/retail/our%20insights/state%20of%20fashion/2023/the-state-of-fashion-2023-holding-onto-growth-as-global-clouds-gathers-vf.pdf`. (Accessed July 7, 2023).

BOF Team and McKinsey & Company (2023). The Year Ahead: What a Fashion Company Looks like in 2023. [online] The Business of Fashion. Available at `www.businessoffashion.com/articles/workplace-talent/the-state-of-fashion-2023-report-organisation-workplace-talent-strategy/` [Accessed Feb. 3, 2023].

Briedis, H., Kronschnabl, A., Rodriguez, A. and Ungerman, K. (2020). Adapting to the next Normal in Retail: the Customer Experience Imperative. [online] Mckinsey. Available at `www.mckinsey.com/industries/retail/our-insights/adapting-to-the-next-normal-in-retail-the-customer-experience-imperative` [Accessed Oct. 8, 2022].

Briggs, J. and Kodnani, D. (2023). The Potentially Large Effects of Artificial Intelligence on Economic Growth. Available at `www.key4biz.it/wp-content/uploads/2023/03/Global-Economics-Analyst_-The-Potentially-Large-Effects-of-Artificial-Intelligence-on-Economic-Growth-Briggs_Kodnani.pdf` (Accessed April 1, 2023).

Bringé, A. (2022). Council Post: How Fashion Brands Can Enter the Metaverse. [online] Forbes. Available at `www.forbes.com/sites/forbescommunicationscouncil/2022/07/01/how-fashion-brands-can-enter-the-metaverse/` [Accessed Nov. 1, 2023].

BIBLIOGRAPHY

Brown, H. (2023). Body Scanning & Size Recommendations Considering Discrepancies. Interviewed by Von N. Ruzive (Google Meet), Feb. 8.

Buchholz, K. (2022). Infographic: The Luxury Brands Selling Luxury NFTs. [online] Statista Infographics. Available at www.statista.com/chart/26869/luxury-fashion-nfts/ [Accessed Feb. 2, 2023].

Business of Fashion and McKinsey & Company (2022). The Year Ahead: Can New Production Models Help Fashion Overcome Supply Chain Woes?. Available at www.businessoffashion.com/articles/retail/the-state-of-fashion-2023-report-supply-chain-manufacturing-nearshoring-vertical-integration/ (Accessed June 6, 2023).

Butler-Young, S. (2023). Why Fashion Should Recruit from outside the Industry. [online] The Business of Fashion. Available at www.businessoffashion.com/articles/workplace-talent/why-fashion-should-recruit-from-outside-the-industry/.

Butte, B. (2015). Cloud: The Engine of the Omni-channel Customer Experience. Available at www.networkworld.com/article/3011910/cloud-the-engine-of-the-omni-channel-customer-experience.html (Accessed October 13, 2023).

Cappasity (2023). Cappasity is the platform for production of immersive shopping experiences. [online] Cappasity. Available at https://cappasity.com/?gad=1&gclid=CjOKCQjwldKmBhCC ARIsAP-OrfyStVidpIlE_ZaGlmZQxI2el9sX1Koi6II3M9Os5fFss ux-3lAEohsaAtjvEALw_wcB (Accessed May 10, 2023).

Cappasity (2022). Top Five Fashion Brands Generating the Most Revenue from NFTs. Available at https://medium.com/cappasity-blog/top-five-fashion-brands-generating-the-most-revenue-from-nfts-26f53f685f51 (Accessed October 13, 2023).

CB Insights (2022). The Future of Fashion: From design to merchandising, how tech is reshaping the industry. Available at www.cbinsights.com/research/report/fashion-tech-future-trends/ (Accessed June 5, 2022).

Cenaro (2021). Showrooming: a Trend Challenging the Retail. [online] blog.cenareo.com. Available at: https://blog.cenareo.com/en/showrooming-bouscule-retail [Accessed 12 Aug. 2022].

Cesareo, S. and White, J. (2023). The Global AI Index. [online] Tortoise. Available at www.tortoisemedia.com/intelligence/global-ai/ [Accessed July 2, 2023].

Chippindale, J. (2022). Holition. Interviewed by Peter Jeun Ho Tsang, October 18.

Clear Fashion (2019). Inform Consumers about the Origin and Impact of Clothing. [online] L'app pour mieux choisir ses vêtements. Available at www.clear-fashion.com/.

Conti, S. (2021). Marine Serre Talks Tech, Textiles and Her Eclectic Approach to Fashion. [online] WWD. Available at wwd.com/feature/marine-serre-talks-tech-textiles-eclectic-approach-fashion-1234853188/ [Accessed Nov. 12, 2022].

Danica, L. (2022). Amazon Opens Its First Fashion Store in Los Angeles. [online] Fast Company. Available at www.fastcompany.com/90755590/amazon-fashion-store-los-angeles (Accessed October 14, 2023).

Data iku (2023). Using ChatGPT, GPT-4, & Large Language Models in the Enterprise. [online] Available at https://blog.dataiku.com/using-chatgpt-llms-in-dataiku.

Demopoulos, Alaina (2023). The Guardian: Computer-generated Inclusivity: Fashion Turns to 'Deiverse' AI Models. Available at www.theguardian.com/fashion/2023/apr/03/ai-virtual-models-fashion-brands (accessed June 20, 2023).

Dishman, L. (2015). Inside LA's new, futuristic store – magic mirrors included. [online] Fortune. Available at https://fortune.com/2015/10/08/rebecca-minkoff-technology/ [Accessed Nov. 12, 2022].

Dixon, S. (2022). Global average time spent per day on social media by generation 2021. [online] Statista. Available at www.statista.com/statistics/1314973/global-daily-time-spent-on-social-media-networks-generation/.

Dogadkina, O. (2023). Emperia. Interviewed by Peter Jeun Ho Tsang, May 16.

Drinkwater, M. (2022). Fashion Innovation Agency. Interviewed by Peter Jeun Ho Tsang, October 18.

Economist Impact (2022). Data point: the case for circular and regenerative fashion. Available at https://impact.economist.com/sustainability/circular-economies/data-point-3-the-case-for-circular-and-regenerative-fashion (Accessed February 9, 2023).

Ellen MacArthur Foundation (2023). Fashion and the Circular Economy Deep Dive. Available at https://ellenmacarthurfoundation.org/fashion-and-the-circular-economy-deep-dive#:~:text=By%20moving%20to%20a%20circular,keep%20safe%20materials%20in%20use (Accessed March 24, 2023).

Fashion Revolution (2023). Definition. Available at www.fashionrevolution.org/definitions/#G (Accessed May 10, 2023).

Fashion United (2014). Report: long queues causes retailers 1 billion in losses. Available at https://fashionunited.uk/v1/fashion/report-long-queues-cause-retailers-1-bn-in-losses/2014031813243 (Accessed May 1, 2023).

Fashion United (2023). Global Fashion Industry Statistics. Available at https://fashionunited.com/global-fashion-industry-statistics (Accessed May 3, 2023).

Foundation, H. (2022). Merging fashion with tech to build a circular economy. [online] H&M Foundation. Available at https://hmfoundation.com/2022/04/25/merging-fashion-with-tech-to-build-a-circular-economy/ [Accessed May 12, 2023].

Francotte, D. (2023). Treedy's. Interviewed by Peter Jeun Ho Tsang (Zoom), February 28.

Gaffié, A. (2020). Pangaia Is The Sustainable Fashion Brand Taking Over Instagram | L'Officiel France. [online] www.lofficielsingapore.com.

Available at www.lofficielsingapore.com/fashion/pangia-life-size-fashion [Accessed Nov. 12, 2022].

Galeries Lafayette (2019). Galeries Lafayette Champs Elysees – A Whole Realm of Possibilities. [online] Available at https://static1.squarespace.com/static/5c9b3eafd74562d4deb03335/t/5ca3319 49b747a60a5ec35e4/1554198946235/Galeries+Lafayette+Champs-Elyse%CC%81es+Essential+2019.pdf (Accessed October 14, 2023).

Galich, K. (2023). Virtual Fitting Room Experience. Interviewed by Von N. Ruzive (Zoom), June 13.

Ganbold, S. (2022). Asia: intention of affluent consumers on purchasing NFTs 2022. [online] Statista. Available at www.statista.com/statistics/1311390/asia-intention-of-affluent-consumers-on-purchasing-nfts/ [Accessed Aug. 2, 2023].

Gartner (2022). Metaverse Hype to Transition into New Business Models that Extend Digital Business. Available at www.gartner.com/en/newsroom/press-releases/2022-02-07-gartner-predicts-25-percent-of-people-will-spend-at-least-one-hour-per-day-in-the-metaverse-by-2026 (Accessed March 24, 2023).

Gokal, K. (2019). Store of the Future: Revolutionising Luxury Retail One Store at a Time - Product - Blog - F-Tech. [online] F-Tech. Available at https://farfetchtechblog.com/en/blog/post/store-of-the-future-revolutionising-luxury-retail-one-store-at-a-time/.

Gonzalo, A., Harreis, H., Sanchez Altable, C., and Villepelet, C. (2020). The Fashion Industry's Digital transformation: Now or Never | McKinsey. [online] McKinsey & Company. Available at www.mckinsey.com/industries/retail/our-insights/fashions-digital-transformation-now-or-never [Accessed Mar. 2, 2022].

Graduate Fashion Week (2022). About Us. Available at www.graduatefashionweek.com/about-us/ (Accessed June 23, 2022).

Granskog, A., Lee, L., Magnus, K.H., and Sawers, C. (2020). Survey: Consumer Sentiment on Sustainability in Fashion. [online] McKinsey & Company. Available at www.mckinsey.com/industries/retail/our-insights/survey-consumer-sentiment-on-sustainability-in-fashion.

Groupe Galeries Lafayette (2019). Our Brands. [online] Galeries Lafayette Group. Available at www.groupegalerieslafayette.com/brands.

Guesné, P. (2022). Refact. Interviewed by Peter Jeun Ho Tsang, (Zoom) 7th December 2022.

Guinebault, M. (2017). Stella McCartney: 'Fashion Production Is Frankly Rather medieval'. [online] Fashion Network. Available at: https://ww.fashionnetwork.com/news/Stella-mccartney-fashion-production-is-frankly-rather-medieval-,876285.html [Accessed Oct. 5, 2022].

Guinebault, M. (2023). Is There a Future for Digital Product Passports in the Fashion and Luxury industry? [online] Fashion Network. Available at https://ww.fashionnetwork.com/news/Is-there-a-future-for-digital-product-passports-in-the-fashion-and-luxury-industry-,1503685.html#marimekko [Accessed Jun. 5, 2023].

Guinebault, M. (2023). Is There a Future for Digital Product Passports in the Fashion and Luxury industry? [online] Fashion Network. Available at https://ww.fashionnetwork.com/news/Is-there-a-future-for-digital-product-passports-in-the-fashion-and-luxury-industry-,1503685.html#tg-botanical.

Hillary, L. (2023). FIT:MATCH.ai with Von N. Ruzive (Via Email), June 20.

Halliday, S. (2018). YSL Opens Interactive Beauty pop-up at Heathrow. [online] Fashion Network. Available at https://ww.fashionnetwork.com/news/ysl-opens-interactive-beauty-pop-up-at-heathrow,905038.html#deadwood [Accessed Aug. 12, 2023].

Harreis, H., Koullias, T., Roberts, R., and Te, K. (2023). Generative AI in Fashion. [online] McKinsey. Available at www.mckinsey.com/industries/retail/our-insights/generative-ai-unlocking-the-future-of-fashion [Accessed Jun. 6, 2023].

Held, C. (2023). Shoefitr Foot Scanning & Recommendations. Interviewed by Von N. Ruzive (Zoom), April 4.

Herget, A. (2022). FINDS. Interviewed by Von N. Ruzive and Peter Jeun Ho Tsang, November 21.

Hill, C. (2023). Inspire Circular. Interviewed by Peter Jeun Ho Tsang (Zoom), May 19.

Holition (2012). Uniqlo | World's First Magic Mirror. [online] holition. com. Available at https://holition.com/work/uniqlo-world-s-first-magic-mirror [Accessed Nov. 12, 2022].

IBM (2023). What is Machine Learning? [online] www.ibm.com. Available at www.ibm.com/topics/machine-learning.

IMRG, Rebound (2023). Report: Navigating the Returns Challenge: A Retailer's Guide. London: IMRG.

Joshi, S. (2023). 58 Augmented Reality Statistics to Unveil AR's Growth. Available at https://learn.g2.com/augmented-reality-statistics (Accessed October 13, 2023).

Iris Van herpen (n.d.). Timeline | about. [online] Iris Van Herpen. Available at www.irisvanherpen.com/about/timeline#:~:text=2010 [Accessed Sep. 12, 2022].

Kansara, V.A. (2017). Inside Farfetch's Store of the Future. [online] The Business of Fashion. Available at www.businessoffashion.com/articles/technology/inside-farfetchs-store-of-the-future/ [Accessed May 16, 2023].

Kansara, V.A. (2017). Inside Farfetch's Store of the Future. [online] The Business of Fashion. Available at www.businessoffashion.com/articles/technology/inside-farfetchs-store-of-the-future/.

Keenan, M. (2022). How Augmented Reality (AR) Is Changing Ecommerce Shopping as We Know It. [online] Shopify Plus. Available at www.shopify.com/enterprise/augmented-reality-ecommerce-shopping.

Khanwala, M. (2023). MishiPay. Interviewed by Peter Jeun Ho Tsang (Zoom), March 28.

Kloss, K. (2022). Karlie Kloss: "Fashion designers in the future won't just be sewing, they'll be coding." [online] CNN. Available at https://edition.cnn.com/style/article/karlie-kloss-september-issues/index.html (Accessed October 14, 2023).

Kloss, K. (2022). Karlie Kloss: Fashion Designers In The Future Won't Just Be Sewing, They'll Be Coding. Available at www.bls.gov/ooh/arts-and-design/fashion-designers.htm#tab-6 (Accessed October 31, 2022).

L'ORÉAL GROUPE (n.d.). L'Oréal's Modiface Brings AI-powered Virtual Makeup Try-on To Amazon. [online] L'Oréal. Available at www.loreal.com/en/articles/science-and-technology/l-oreal-modiface-brings-ai-powered-virtual-makeup-try-ons-to-amazon/ [Accessed Nov. 12, 2022].

Lablaco (2021). lablaco – fashion made circular. [online] www.lablaco.com. Available at www.lablaco.com/.

Langenheim, J. (2015). A Scrap of difference: Why Fashion Offcuts don't Need to End up in Landfill. [online] National Geographic. Available at www.nationalgeographic.com/environment/article/partner-content-prada-renylon-ganzhou-china.

Lau, J. (2022). London College of Fashion. Interviewed by Peter Jeun Ho Tsang, October 25.

Launchmart (n.d.). Drippy - Fashion design made easy. [online] www.drippyapp.com. Available at www.drippyapp.com/ [Accessed Aug. 10, 2023].

Lee, I. (2021). Markets Insider: Luxury NFTs could become a $56 billion market by 2030 and could see 'dramatically' increased demand thanks to the metaverse. Available at https://markets.businessinsider.com/news/currencies/luxury-nfts-metaverse-56-billion-market-revenue-2030-morgan-stanley-2021-11 (Accessed June 7, 2023).

Levine, A. (2022). Interviewed by Peter Jeun Ho Tsang, September 23.

Licata, M. and Kemp, W. (2020). The Future of Work in Fashion. [online] UN Today. Available at https://untoday.org/the-future-of-work-in-fashion/ [Accessed Sep. 1, 2022].

Lo, D. (2022). Amazon Opens Its First Fashion Store in Los Angeles. [online] www.fastcompany.com. Available at www.fastcompany.com/90755590/amazon-fashion-store-los-angeles.

M&S (n.d.). M&S Acquires Thread IP to Accelerate Its Personalisation Plans. [online] Marks & Spencer. Available at https://corporate.marksandspencer.com/media/press-releases/ms-acquires-thread-ip-accelerate-its-personalisation-plans.

Mack, K., Hsu, R.C.L., Monroy-Hernández, A., Smith, B.A., and Liu, F. (2023). Towards Inclusive Avatars: Disability Representation in Avatar Platforms. Proceedings of the 2023 CHI Conference on Human Factors in Computing Systems. [online] doi: https://doi.org/10.1145/3544548.3581481.

Maguire, L. (2021). Balenciaga launches on Fortnite: What it means for luxury. [online] Vogue Business. Available at www.voguebusiness.com/technology/balenciaga-launches-on-fortnite-what-it-means-for-luxury [Accessed May 14, 2023].

Manning, E. (2016). five archival fashion tech moments, from andré courrèges to alexander mcqueen. [online] i-d.vice.com. Available at https://i-d.vice.com/en/article/wj59m5/five-archival-fashion-tech-moments-from-andr-courrges-to-alexander-mcqueen [Accessed Apr. 12, 2023].

Mcdowell, M. (2019). Tommy Hilfiger switches to 100% digital design. [online] Vogue Business. Available at www.voguebusiness.com/technology/tommy-hilfiger-pvh-corp-3d-design-digital-clothing-innovation-sustainability [Accessed Feb. 1, 2023].

Mcdowell, M. (2023). Google Introduces Virtual try-on Using Generative AI. [online] Vogue Business. Available at www.voguebusiness.com/technology/google-introduces-virtual-try-on-using-generative-ai [Accessed June 13, 2022].

Mcdowell, M. and Schulz, M. (2023). The Vogue Business NFT Tracker. [online] Vogue Business. Available at www.voguebusiness.com/technology/the-vogue-business-nft-tracker [Accessed Mar. 8, 2023].

McKinsey & Company (2022). State of Fashion Technology Report 2022. Available at http://www.mckinsey.com/industries/retail/our-insights/state-of-fashion-technology-report-2022 (Accessed October 13, 2023).

Meta (2022). Why We Still Believe in the Future. Available at https://tech.facebook.com/reality-labs/2022/12/boz-look-back-2023-look-ahead/ (Accessed October 13, 2023).

Mihić, M., Anić, I.-D., and Kursan Milaković, I. (2018). Time Spent Shopping and Consumer Clothing Purchasing Behaviour. Ekonomski Pregled. [online] 69(2). doi: https://doi.org/10.32910/ep.69.2.1.

Minina, E. (2023). 3D Interactive Shopping Experiences. Interviewed by Von N. Ruzive (Zoom), June 16.

N-Hega (n.d.). Pattern Digitizing Systems/Pattern Digitizers: Scanner & Camera Digitizer. [online] N-Hega - Pattern Digitizers & Pattern Digitizing. Available at www.n-hega.com/ [Accessed Aug. 10, 2023].

Nguyen, T. (2023). Digital Design & 3D Builder. Interviewed by Von N. Ruzive (Zoom), Apr. 4.

Nikolay Anguelov (2021). The Sustainable Fashion Quest: Innovations in Business and Policy. New York: Productivity Press.

NOKIA & IPSOS (2022). Gen Z and the metaverse: A multi-market study on how Gen Z currently experience the metaverse and the role they want to play in its future.

Office For National Statistics (2022). Disabled people's Experiences with activities, Goods and services, UK - Office for National Statistics. [online] www.ons.gov.uk. Available at www.ons.gov.uk/peoplepopulationandcommunity/healthandsocialcare/disability/bulletins/disabledpeoplesexperienceswithactivitiesgoodsandservicesuk/februarytomarch2022.

Paris Good Fashion (2022). France: Clothes will have to mention a new information #398. [online] Paris Good Fashion. Available at https://parisgoodfashion.fr/en/news/france-clothes-will-have-to-mention-a-new-information-398/ (Accessed October 14, 2023).

Phelps, N. (2019). Louis Vuitton's New Capsule with League of Legends Brings French High Fashion to Online Gaming—and Vice Versa. [online] Vogue. Available at www.vogue.com/article/louis-vuittons-new-capsule-with-league-of-legends [Accessed Feb. 3, 2023].

Polet, AC. (2022). Stitch. Interviewed by Peter Jeun Ho Tsang (Zoom), October 28.

Porter, J. (2022). Amazon's First Clothing Store Lets You Summon Clothes to the Fitting Room. [online] The Verge. Available at https://www.theverge.com/2022/1/20/22892880/amazon-style-fashion-apperal-retail-los-angeles-fitting-room.

PVH (2022). Tommy Hilfiger Introduces 'Tommy Factory': a Warhol-Inspired Creative Playground, Coming This Fall. [online] www.pvh.com. Available at www.pvh.com/news/tommy-factory [Accessed Mar. 12, 2023].

Ramachandran, R. (2022). QBrics. Interviewed by Peter Jeun Ho Tsang (Zoom), December 13.

RFID Card (2020). UNIQLO has Rolled Out RFID Technology. [online] RFID Card. Available at www.rfidcard.com/uniqlo-has-rolled-out-rfid-technology/ [Accessed June 3, 2022].

Richter, F. (2018). Infographic: Baby Boomers Embrace Technology. [online] Statista Infographics. Available at www.statista.com/chart/13206/device-ownership-among-baby-boomers/.

Rodriguez Cife, A. (2021). New FTAlliance report unveils the 8 key future jobs in fashion-tech. Available at www.arts.ac.uk/knowledge-exchange/stories/new-report-unveils-8-future-jobs-in-fashion-tech (Accessed June 23, 2022).

Rogovskiy, V. (2022). 3D Look. Interviewed by Peter Jeun Ho Tsang (Zoom), November 15.

Romero, N. (2022). Futures Factory. Interviewed by Peter Jeun Ho Tsang (Zoom), October 4, 2022.

RTFKT (2023). Available at https://rtfkt.com/ (Accessed June 5, 2023).

Sabanoglu, T. (2023). UK: AR/VR dressing rooms impact on online luxury sales. [online] Statista. Available at www.statista.com/statistics/1288521/ar-vr-dressing-room-effect-on-online-luxury-sales-uk/ [Accessed Jul. 30, 2023].

Schwab, K. (2017). The Fourth Industrial Revolution. London: Penguin Books Limited.

Seelig, IM. (2022). AnamXR. Interviewed by Peter Jeun Ho Tsang (Zoom), October 19.

Shah, S. (2022). AltMat. Interviewed by Peter Jeun Ho Tsang (Zoom), December 16, 2022.

Shorman, A. (2022). More Options, More Platforms and Super Bowl LVI Shirts for Avatars. [online] Meta. Available at https://about.fb.com/news/2022/01/updates-to-avatars/ [Accessed Oct. 7, 2022].

Smartzer (2023). Available at www.smartzer.com// (Accessed June 6, 2023).

Smith, P. (2022). Global Adaptive Apparel Market Size 2019-2025. [online] Statista. Available at www.statista.com/statistics/875613/global-adaptive-apparel-market-size/.

Smith, P. (2022a). Artificial Intelligence in the Global Fashion Market Value 2027. [online] Statista. Available at www.statista.com/statistics/1070736/global-artificial-intelligence-fashion-market-size/ [Accessed Jan. 2, 2023].

Smith, P. (2022b). Global Adaptive Apparel Market Size 2019-2025. [online] Statista. Available at www.statista.com/statistics/875613/global-adaptive-apparel-market-size/ [Accessed Feb. 13, 2023].

Smith, P. (2023). Women's Plus-size Apparel Market in the U.S. [online] Statista. Available at www.statista.com/topics/4834/women-s-plus-size-apparel-market-in-the-us/#topicOverview [Accessed Aug. 5, 2022].

SNAP Inc. X Ipsos (2022). Augmentality Shift U.S. Report. [online] Available at `https://downloads.ctfassets.net/inb32lme5009/4xk5qWu hFbSOhJiMSTqxd2/85044c43ecc8c051cffe8320ee715804/Augmentality_ Shift_US_2022.pdf` (Accessed October 14, 2023).

Snapchat (2019). Snapchat - The fastest way to share a moment! [online] Snapchat.com. Available at `www.snapchat.com/`.

Snapchat (2020). Gucci | Snapchat for Business. [online] forbusiness. snapchat.com. Available at `https://forbusiness.snapchat.com/ inspiration/gucci-ar-tryon` (Accessed October 14, 2023).

Statista Research Department (2023). Global: e-commerce Fashion Sales Share by Region. [online] Statista. Available at `www.statista.com/ forecasts/1305339/e-commerce-fashion-sales-channel-by-region- worldwide` [Accessed Aug. 1, 2023].

Statista (2023). Fashion E-Commerce Worldwide - Statistics & Facts. Available at `www.statista.com/topics/9288/fashion-e-commerce- worldwide/#topicOverview` (Accessed June 6, 2023).

Statista (2023). Most Returned Online Purchases by Category in the UK as of March 2023. Available at `www.statista.com/forecasts/997848/ most-returned-online-purchases-by-category-in-the-uk` (Accessed June 20, 2023).

Statista (2023). Number of internet and social media users worldwide as of April 2023. Available at `www.statista.com/statistics/617136/ digital-population-worldwide/#:~:text=Worldwide%20digital%20 population%202023&text=As%20of%20April%202023%2C%20there, population%2C%20were%20social%20media%20users` (Accessed August 8, 2023).

Stella McCartney (n.d.). Recycled nylon and polyester | Stella McCartney FR. [online] `www.stellamccartney.com`. Available at `www. stellamccartney.com/fr/fr/sustainability/recycled-nylon- polyester.html` [Accessed June 12, 2023].

BIBLIOGRAPHY

Stella McCartney (n.d.). Stella McCartney × UNECE Blockchain Technology Pilot. [online] www.stellamccartney.com. Available at www.stellamccartney.com/mc/fr/stellas-world/our-unece-block-chain-pilot-paves-the-way-for-more-responsible-sourcing.html [Accessed June 12, 2023].

Stitch Fix (2022). Stitch Fix Announces Fourth Quarter and Fiscal Year 2022 Financial Results. Available at https://investors.stitchfix.com/news-releases/news-release-details/stitch-fix-announces-fourth-quarter-and-fiscal-year-2022 (Accessed October 13, 2023).

T-Fashion (2022). T-Fashion | Fashion Trend Forecasting Meets Artificial Intelligence. [online] tfashion.ai. Available at https://tfashion.ai/.

The Fabricant (2023). Our Mission. Available at www.thefabricant.com/about (Accessed June 5, 2023).

thredUP (2023). Resale Report 2023. Available at https://cf-assets-tup.thredup.com/resale_report/2023/thredUP_2023_Resale%20Report_Executive%20Summary.pdf (Accessed May 15, 2023).

Tracxn (2023). Fashion Tech. Available at https://tracxn.com/d/sectors/fashion-tech/__53qhEF-ggugleKVAdyOnOEuiYuYLFAxsYSbDGem-p4o (Accessed June 20, 2023).

U.S. Bureau of Labor Statistics (2022). Fashion Designers. Available at www.bls.gov/ooh/arts-and-design/fashion-designers.htm#tab-6 (Accessed June 23, 2022).

Unidays (2022). 2022 Sustainability Report: Should Fashion's Last Mile Go Green for Gen Z?. Available at https://4000540.fs1.hubspotusercontent-na1.net/hubfs/4000540/UNiDAYS%20Sustainability%20Report%202022%20x%20Zedify.pdf (Accessed May 31, 2023).

Van Elven, M. (2018). Fashion United: Infographic: the extent of overproduction in the fashion industry. Available at https://fashionunited.uk/news/fashion/infographic-the-extent-of-overproduction-in-the-fashion-industry/2018121240500 (Accessed February 9, 2023).

Vanhoeck, C. (2022). Resortecs. Interviewed by Peter Jeun Ho Tsang (Zoom), December 5, 2022.

Vogue Business Data & Insights Team (2021). Resale, Rental and NFTs: Vogue Business Index Reveals Top Trends in Innovation. [online] Vogue Business. Available at www.voguebusiness.com/companies/resale-rental-nft-vogue-business-index-trends-innovation [Accessed Feb. 1, 2023].

WANNA (n.d.). Digital Transformation Expert for Luxury Brands. [online] wanna.fashion. Available at https://wanna.fashion/.

WANNA (n.d.). WANNA SNEAKERS TRY-ON. [online] wanna.fashion. Available at https://wanna.fashion/sneakers-try-on [Accessed Mar.12, 2023].

Warmerdam, K. (2023). Transparency At AWARE. Interviewed by Von N. Ruzive (Zoom), January 20.

Wilders, C. (2023). OuttaWRLD. Interviewed by Peter Jeun Ho Tsang (Zoom), March 30, 2023.

World Health Organization (2023). Disability and Health. [online] www.who.int. Available at www.who.int/news-room/fact-sheets/detail/disability-and-health#:~:text=Key%20facts.

Yeung, E. (2023). Pattern Digitizing. Interviewed by Von N. Ruzive (Zoom), January 31, 2023.

Yeung, K. (2022). Microsoft. Interviewed by Peter Jeun Ho Tsang (Zoom), November 22, 2022.

Yeung, K. (2023). Incubation and On-demand Manufacturing. Interviewed by Von N. Ruzive (Zoom), June 13, 2023.

Yu, R. (2023). Digital Fashion Design Software. Interviewed by Von N. Ruzive (Zoom), Jan 5.

Index

A

Adaptive fashion, 184
Adobe Illustrator, 39
AGEC law, 158, 159
AI digital size recommendation
    solution, 184
AI-generated models, 223
AI-powered image creation
    platform, 222
AI-powered personalization
    tools, 192
AI virtual try-ons, 184
AltMat, 96
    agricultural waste, 72
    biorefinery, 74
    fabricating material
        innovation, 72
    fibers into yarns, 73
    garments, 74
    innovation progress, 74
    next-generation materials, 76
    waste into fabric, 73
Amazon Style store, 6
Analytical platforms, 64
AnamXR, 143, 145–148
Anne-Christine Polet, 135
Anne-Christine's intrapreneurial
    solution, 221
Anti-waste law for a circular
    economy (AGEC), 89
AR digital fashion, 205
Artificial intelligence (AI), 3,
    18, 43, 191
AR virtual try-on function, 134, 180
Augmented reality (AR), 54,
    204, 205
    collaboration, 119
    description, 113
    holograms, 118, 119
    immersion, 115
    interactivity, 119
    movement tracking, 115
    3DLOOK, 122
    virtual try-on feature, 116, 118
Authentication process, 92
Autonomous delivery vehicles
    (ADV), 190

B

Back-end infrastructure, 155
Back-end technologies, 23, 24
B2C retail, 206

O

P

Printed in the United States
by Baker & Taylor Publisher Services